The World of
Wildlife

The World of
Wildlife

Published in collaboration with the World Wildlife Fund

Edited by Nigel Sitwell

Hamlyn
London · New York · Sydney · Toronto

Previous page: alert swamp
deer (southern race) in the
Kanha National Park in India.
Despite its name, this deer
favors a grassy plain as its
habitat. It has declined in
number from 3000 forty years
ago to barely a hundred today

First published in Great Britain in 1977 by
THE HAMLYN PUBLISHING GROUP LIMITED
London · New York · Sydney · Toronto
Astronaut House, Feltham,
Middlesex, England

This book has been designed and produced by
London Editions Limited
30 Uxbridge Road, London W12 8ND

ISBN: 0 600 39391 7

Printed and bound in Great Britain

While it is intended that the information and opinions
expressed in this book reflect the policies of the World
Wildlife Fund and its sister organization, the
International Union for Conservation of Nature and
Natural Resources, the contents are the responsibility of
the various contributors and the editor.

CONTRIBUTORS

Nigel Sitwell Editor, *Wildlife Magazine*
Thor Heyerdahl
Robert Allen Science Writer, IUCN
Peter Jackson Director of Information, World Wildlife Fund International
Kenneth Whitehead Deer Group, Survival Service Commission, IUCN
David Black Staff Biologist, World Wildlife Fund, Britain
Dr Yoshinori Imaizumi
Dr Robert Stebbing
Michael Everett Royal Society for the Protection of Birds
Ken and Marilyn Poertner
Hans Beste
Erwin Bauer
Tony Loftas Marine Consultant, *New Scientist*
Randall Reeves
Robert Rush Miller Professor of Zoology, University of Michigan
John A. Burton Assistant Secretary, Fauna Preservation Society
Dr M. R. K. Lambert Acting Secretary, British Herpetological Society
Anthony Strubell

ACKNOWLEDGEMENTS

Cover J. Seager/British Antarctic Survey; 2–3 J.-P. Ferrero; 9 Rita Wüthrich; 16 Bruce Coleman; 17 Nicholas Devore/Bruce Coleman; 18 François Gohier; 19 Jeff Foott/
Bruce Coleman; 21 John Wallis/Bruce Coleman, C. B. Frith/Bruce Coleman; 22 Norman Myers/Bruce Coleman, Jeff Foott/Bruce Coleman; 23 Norman Tomalin/Bruce Coleman,
K. & D. Urry/Bruce Coleman; 26 Peter Jackson; 27 Ch. Zuber/World Wildlife Fund; 28 J.-P. Ferrero; 29 P. Castel/Jacana; 30 R. Idzerda/World Wildlife Fund, Project Tiger/
World Wildlife Fund; 32–33 Francisco Erize/Bruce Coleman; 36–37 J.-P. Ferrero; 38 Philippa Scott, D. R. McCullough/World Wildlife Fund; 40 G. K. Whitehead; 41 George B.
Schaller/Bruce Coleman, Peter Jackson/Bruce Coleman, David Hughes/Bruce Coleman; 42–43 J. Trotignon/Jacana; 44 Jane Burton/Bruce Coleman; 45 J. Trotignon/Jacana;
46 World Wildlife Fund, Francisco Erize/Bruce Coleman; 48–52 Tadaaki Imaizumi & Tetsuo Chabata; 54–55 S. C. Bisserot; 57 R. E. Stebbings; 58–59 S. C. Bisserot/Bruce
Coleman; 60 S. C. Bisserot, John M. Burnley/Bruce Coleman; 61 S. C. Bisserot/Bruce Coleman; 64–65 P. van Groenendael & W. Suetens; 66 Derek Middleton/Bruce Coleman;
67 top and centre Gordon Langsbury/Bruce Coleman, bottom RSPB; 68–70 Joseph van Wormer/Bruce Coleman; 71 Jan & Des Bartlett/Bruce Coleman; 72–73 Charlie Ott/
Bruce Coleman; 74–77 Hans & Judy Beste; 79 Graham Pizzey; 81 Hans & Judy Beste; 85–86 Fred Bruemmer; 87 Philippa Scott; 89 Tom Nebbia/Aspect Picture Library;
90 Ian Collinge/British Antarctic Survey; 93 Nigel Merrett/Seaphot; 95 Crown Copyright; 96–97 D. Lusby/Sea Library; 100 Fred Bruemmer, Tierbilder Okapia; 102–103 Alan M.
Heller; 104–105 Dr R. R. Miller; 107–109 Alan M. Heller; 111 A. R. Devez/Jacana; 112–113 J.-P. Ferrero; 114 S. C. Bisserot; 115 John Andrew Burton, R. Volot/Jacana;
117 S. C. Bisserot; 119 Heather Angel; 121 A. Strubel; 122 Heather Angel; 123 Juan Solaro/Jacana; 124–125 Heather Angel; 126 A. Strubel; 127 Sigurd Halvorsen/Bruce
Coleman; 128 R. Tory Peterson/Bruce Coleman; 131–132 Peter Jackson/World Wildlife Fund; 133 Thor Larsen/World Wildlife Fund; 134 I. Douglas-Hamilton/World Wildlife
Fund; 135 Rolf Bengtssen/World Wildlife Fund; 136 Dolder/World Wildlife Fund; 137 World Scout Bureau; 139 E. Zimen and Luigi Boitani/World Wildlife Fund.

CONTENTS

INTRODUCTION

by Nigel Sitwell

Dedicated conservationists are used to answering a number of basic questions. These tend to be simple and fundamental, but despite the fact that the need for wildlife conservation seems the most obvious thing in the world, to those who believe in it, these questions are curiously difficult to answer in as simple a form as they are posed. Britain's Prince Philip once made an oblique reference to this difficulty when he said that anyone who questioned the need for conservation would not understand the answer! But of course, in practise, one has to search for answers that can be understood by everyone—and that is what I find myself doing quite frequently.

One of these basic questions goes something like this. If an animal species has apparently never been particularly abundant, and is now reduced to a tiny remnant population, is it worth spending a lot of effort and money on keeping it in existence? Especially if, because of widespread changes to or destruction of its habitat, it is never likely to recover to more than a fraction of its former population. What possible role is this species now playing in the ecosystem—and what role could it ever play, given that vigilant protection (which costs money) will probably always be necessary to maintain its population even in small numbers?

There is always something that scientists can learn from such species, something that may well be of value in the study and understanding of other species. But an interesting and important reason for conserving these animals can be expressed in the phrase 'public relations'. They can become symbols for the many millions of people who know little or nothing of conservation; they can represent the dire problems facing all wildlife; they can play a decisive educational role in the battle to save wild animals and wild places. It helps, undoubtedly, that these seriously reduced species are often large or spectacular creatures.

I well remember travelling to the island of Bawean in the Java Sea in 1969 and re-discovering (as far as the outside world was concerned) the handsome little Bawean deer which Kenneth Whitehead discusses in his article in this book on endangered deer. The animal had probably never lived anywhere else but on this one small island in historical times—and as the island's human population expanded, it was clear that if nothing were done the deer would gradually be driven to extinction through sheer

Nigel Sitwell during a seafishing expedition off the Gulf coast of Texas

competition for living space. The late Hilmi Oesman, an Indonesian conservationist who went with me, tried to persuade the village headmen on the island (with some success I believe) that they should be proud to share their home with a unique animal—one that was found nowhere else in Indonesia, let alone the rest of the world. It was therefore their duty to protect it. This appeal had a strong attraction for the local people, who were relatively poor and isolated, and out of the mainstream of Indonesian life. It gave them pleasure to think that they were the sole guardians of the deer on behalf of the rest of their large nation. It set them apart, even above their fellow countrymen. (I have not been back to the island since then, so I do not know whether our appeal has had a lasting effect, though it certainly seemed to make sense to the islanders at the time.)

The Javan rhino, numbering barely fifty animals and confined to a peninsula on the extreme western tip of Java, and the Mauritius kestrel, which is down to a mere dozen birds on its Indian Ocean island home, are further examples of very rare species. There are two more, which are discussed in this book, and which are perfect examples of the point I am making: the osprey in Scotland and the whooping crane of North America. If one is honest, neither bird has any real effect on the other animals or plants with which it coexists (the osprey is more abundant elsewhere, of course, but I am referring to the Scottish population). It might well make no biological difference if they were to vanish. But many thousands of people travel to see them each year, and a large proportion of these visitors are not already committed conservationists. Having seen a nesting osprey, or the courtship dance of a pair of whooping cranes, it is highly likely that the observer will come away with a new understanding for nature—and an appreciation of the importance of conservation.

These two birds, statistically insignificant though they may be, have a beneficial effect on the natural world that is quite disproportionate to their ecological role. They amply repay every penny or cent that is lavished on their protection.

An ever-present threat to wildlife which is highlighted in this book is the greedy over-exploitation of certain animal species by the pet trade. The desire of human beings to keep wild animals as pets is no new thing—which does not make it easy to conserve those animals which are in demand. The fact is that if there is a demand for something in this world of ours, someone, somewhere is going to try to satisfy the demand, whether it is for golden-shouldered parrots from Australia or baby tortoises from North Africa. It is extremely difficult to control such trade effectively by legislation alone. The only real solution is to bring about a change in attitude.

Once it was fashionable for men to wear elaborate wigs, and there were many wig-makers to meet the demand. But when it became unfashionable for men to wear wigs, nothing the wig-makers could do was any use. Men simply didn't want to wear wigs any more and the wig-makers went out of business. So it is up to animal-lovers and conservationists to lead the way in making it unfashionable to keep wild animals as pets. Only when the demand has dried up will the animal dealers go out of business.

Finally, this book emphasizes the current World Wildlife Fund/IUCN campaign to save the marine environment. Various articles, including Thor Heyerdahl's, focus attention on the problem of what mankind is doing to the seas and oceans. The last great natural environment on our planet that is still relatively intact, the marine world is nevertheless already coming under pressure. Certain food fishes and marine mammals like the great whales are facing severe threats, and some of our seas are becoming grossly polluted.

Much of the 'glamor' of conservation centers around individual animals and plants, but ultimately none of these living things can survive unless we protect their habitat. Mountainous regions, the semi-deserts, and tropical rain forests are a few of the important wildlife habitats which have already attracted attention, and which are increasingly the subject of urgent action-orientated projects. Now it is the turn of the marine environment, perhaps the most important natural treasure left on Planet Earth, and the one that we can least afford to degrade and despoil. This campaign is of the utmost significance: it is hardly an exaggeration to say that our own survival depends on its success. We cannot afford to let it fail.

NATURE AND THE ADVANCE OF MAN

by Thor Heyerdahl

'Progress' is a magic word. It really ought to mean everything that advances—everything that changes into something better. For generations we human beings have been fighting against our environment, trying to get away from the wilds and create a world of our own in which we make all the decisions and animals and plants survive or are eradicated according to our wishes. We have become so sure of ourselves that we have taken it for granted that every change in our original environment that we bring about with our science and technology must necessarily be an improvement on the primitive nature that our ancestors received from Our Lord. And with this self-confident conviction we have until recently never hesitated to use the word 'progress' for everything we have done in the past to take us farther and farther from nature.

This sort of progress has gone so far now that in many countries thoughtful people have begun to react, to remind their fellow men that we may perhaps be going too far, perhaps going the wrong way—that perhaps we ought to preserve some of the original life of the world before it's too late.

One of the many results of this gradual awakening was the establishment of the World Wildlife Fund, which in record time has won the support from active groups in individual countries. Some people think the World Wildlife Fund is a sort of privileged consortium of big game hunters intent on building up a stock of wild animals so that they can still have something to shoot. Even if we suppose that a very small number of the supporters of the movement might have such an idea at the back of their minds, they would still be far preferable to people who turn their backs on nature and couldn't care less if all life outside the city limits disappears. I am not a hunter myself, and thousands of others like me throughout the world support the World Wildlife Fund because we see it as an active, purposeful organization that aims at something positive, that is really *doing* something . . . and that has already done an incredible amount all round the world to preserve animal life and the natural environment for generations to come, in scrupulous cooperation with zoologists and other expert natural scientists.

Why worry about nature? Isn't it sentimental to preserve wildlife in a world where civilization, technology, and culture are the aims? Isn't tomorrow's welfare state going to be an urban community with no weeds, no vermin, only the plants that we choose to grow in parks and gardens, and wild animals adequately displayed as curiosities in cages? Can culture and nature be combined as we enter into the third millennium?

The answer is quite simply that culture and nature cannot be separated. It's the unenlightened savage in us, the medieval fear of a wild world abandoned and unknown, that makes us retreat behind our doors and peer out at nature through the windows as at something foreign that does not really concern us. But the same science, which in its initial stages led us away from nature into the man-made world we inhabit today, is beginning now to perceive the miracle behind the whole of creation, to tell us that mankind is just one part of an inseparable biological partnership, a shoot growing at the top of the trunk yet still entirely dependent on the life of the whole tree as an entity down to the furthest tips of its roots.

No great insight is required to comprehend that human beings did not invent their own lungs or blood system, nor the brain, constructed with such tremendous ingenuity that science is still struggling hard to find out how this most complex of computors functions. All our chromosomes were donated to us by the living things that came before us. It was the wildlife of the woods that furnished us with genes after the plants in the wilderness had produced oxygen and food, permitting our exist-

ence. Whether we believe in Darwin's theory of evolution or the Biblical account of the Creation, no natural force nor any almighty Creator was able to bring forth mankind until all the plants and animals, the whole biological environment, were present. So ingeniously was the whole ecological system built up without any help from man that every last organism had its own particular duty, allowing the global machinery to function and forming part of the truly wondrous life-cycle that distinguishes the earth from the other dead planets and satellites.

Mankind, which has received everything from the natural environment, has for the past five thousand years used its developing civilization to fight and annihilate that very same environment, heedless of future consequences. The earth beneath our feet was in the beginning as dead and empty as the lunar landscape. Life began in the sea. It was in the sea that the first life arose, and that by no mere chance. No creature could begin to crawl or walk on land until life in the sea had, quite literally, made it possible for land animals to draw breath. There were only sterile gases around our planet until the tiny, almost invisible organisms we call marine plankton began the production of oxygen. Endless quantities of nearly microscopic vegetable plankton, phytoplankton, increased and multiplied in the sunlight on the sea's surface and by the process of photosynthesis produced so much oxygen that this gas, essential to life, rose up from the surface of the water and was mixed with the sterile gases until our planet had the atmosphere that is a condition of life for all breathing creatures. Phytoplankton have never ceased this production, and even today the forests on land would not be able, by themselves, to supply all the oxygen consumed by the animal kingdom.

In the primitive communities men would not have cared if the insignificant plankton in the sea had been destroyed, together with ants and worms and mice and any other inedible creatures of the forest. However, we are now beginning to understand how all these apparently superfluous creatures are essential to our very existence. Every one of them produces something we ourselves require, directly or indirectly, or removes something that has to be got rid of or converted if the conditions of life on our planet are to continue indefinitely. Human beings may be compared with the

9

hands on a clock: it is the hands that we look at and take notice of—but all the other parts are there working together like the unseen mechanism which makes the hands move round.

When I was a university student nearly all the emphasis in zoological studies was on anatomy, on analysis in the laboratory of the interior structure of the different animals. But there was a growing interest in the interdependence of the species. We drew graphs showing how predators such as foxes and hawks produced more young as soon as there had been a 'lemming year', with abnormal numbers of small rodents. It was not until the greater number of predators had greatly reduced the numbers of small mammals that the surplus predators died out as a result of the limited amounts of food. In that way the normal populations of foxes and hawks, mice and lemmings were restored. Today increasing numbers of zoologists have undertaken systematic research into this complex ecological system and have pointed out an unwritten law of nature that shows how one species helps to keep another in check so that a general rule of two surviving young operates for all species, whether it is a whale that feeds a single calf at a time or a cod that lays hundreds of thousands of eggs at one spawning.

Man is the first creature that, although himself a part of this same ecological system, has nevertheless managed to break the law of equilibrium. We have contrived to drive other species both up to and also past the limit of extinction, and we have contrived to multiply so enormously at the expense of other species that today there are two billion people suffering from starvation or malnutrition. All this we have achieved with the aid of modern technology, and what is worse, in the wake of this enormous and abnormal human population explosion there has followed a rapidly increasing pollution of the environment.

The animal life around us can be destroyed in so many ways, and we have used them all: thoughtless decimation by excessive hunting and capture; deliberate extermination by poison and spraying; encroachment on important links in the food chain; reduction of the natural habitat by urbanization, communications, and agriculture; and damage by industrial effluents, oil spillage, and the ceaseless leakage of all sorts of new and deadly chemicals

from town and country.

It is in these fields that the World Wildlife Fund is stimulating, firstly, serious studies by competent scientists, and secondly the involvement of states and governments in every relevant sphere. The opportunities are manifold, and as time passes they will increase. To begin with it is a question of creating areas of conservation, nature parks, where the local ecological system can be re-established and maintain itself, to the advantage and enjoyment of peaceful visitors. It is equally important to enact (and enforce) laws in areas outside the nature parks where the balance of nature is already disturbed. There, man must aid the natural ecological processes by artificial means wherever the natural balance has been upset.

Men are spreading today like yeast in wine, no longer at a steady rate of growth but at a lunatic rate that will potentially see the doubling of the world's population in less than each generation. And chemical pollution increases in proportion. I've heard biologists use the simile of yeast in wine in more than one way: the yeast thrives in the grape juice, where it consumes the grape sugar and produces alcohol, multiplying so enormously that the spirit, or pollution, it forms ultimately destroys all life in the grape juice, including that of the yeast itself. It is certain that the incredibly swift decline in animal life in every continent, on every island, in the oceans and lakes, is due to the tremendous expansion and technological development of mankind. The by-products that endless millions of consumers pour into the environment today in the form of indestructible new chemicals, insecticides and weedkillers, disinfectants, hair sprays, exhaust gases, factory smoke, and liquid industrial effluent, in addition to the urbanization of ever more areas and the resultant destruction of the world's last great jungle regions, threaten the surviving animal life far more than hunting and fishing, which are easier to regulate and control. It is not the local fishermen who have killed off thousands of trout in hundreds of Norwegian mountain streams; it is acid smoke from abroad.

The world population of whales will not be threatened by hunting if every country introduces regulations which will allow the whales to increase their numbers to a level that justifies catching; but it will be threatened if the plankton are poisoned. And biologists have already found the first signs that this is a coming problem. As we know, DDT was found a long time ago in the flesh of penguins in the Antarctic and in the brains of polar bears in the Arctic; every one of twenty whales that were caught for biological studies in the polar stream off Greenland were found to have DDT and other insecticides in their blubber. These polar animals don't live anywhere near any agricultural regions, but the marine currents flow all round the world like broad rivers, and with them the drifting plankton. Polluted sea-water circulates through the microscopic digestive apparatus of the plankton, where DDT and other chlorinated hydrocarbons are absorbed into its tissue as if by blotting paper while only the pure sea water passes through. Millions of plankton are eaten by every single fish and every single crustacean, and these in turn are the food of the whales. And the poisons which were originally absorbed by countless numbers of miniscule organisms pass in increased concentration into the food chain until at last men find in the whale the indestructible poisons they had invented merely to be sprayed on their crops to kill insects.

So it is accordingly not very far from the plantlouse and the gnat to the fish and the whale, and mankind sits on top of the ecological pyramid and gets the punishment for damage done to the pyramid's lowest level. The greatest geographical discovery since the ancient Greeks worked out that the world was round, and Columbus and Magellan proved them right, is the observation made in our own time, that our globe is not only round, it is also astonishingly small. You can travel round it in a space-ship in an hour, and in a few weeks you can drift over the biggest ocean in the world on a bundle of reeds. When we did this, on the papyrus vessel *Ra II*, we picked up lumps of tar from the washing-out of oil tankers on 43 of the 57 days that the trans-Atlantic journey from Africa to America lasted. The ocean is deep, but life is concentrated on and just below its surface, and that is where the buoyant, non-convertible poisons remain which nowadays continually float out to sea from every sewer and every river in the world. What is more, the ocean is not as deep as we often think. The length of six supertankers is more than the average depth of most oceans, and if New York was built on the bottom of the North Sea most of the downtown buildings would have more

floors above water than below it.

And what of the great primeval forests of Africa and South America? They are not so big: in our own generation alone more has been cleared from them than is still standing. Civilization makes progress in every part of the world, and we can't stop that, but today more than ever we must try to find out what is genuine progress and what is really a move in the wrong direction. For if civilization is to survive, and with it the human species, then culture and nature must go hand in hand, for today each depends on the other.

THE GREAT WHALES

Modern whales are a group of marine mammals whose ancestors left the land some 100 million years ago, and which are very well adapted for life in the marine environment. There are over thirty kinds of true whales, as well as many more porpoises and dolphins. Whales are intelligent social animals: sounds are important to them for navigation, but they also use very beautiful 'songs' to communicate with each other. Unfortunately these large, friendly animals have been over-exploited by man for many years. The first whaling industry started in the ninth century with the Basques, who hunted the right whale along their coasts. Whaling has since become super-efficient, with the use of sonar to locate the whales, giant factory ships to process the carcasses in the open ocean, and above all the modern harpoon. Once a simple hand-held 'spear', it is now loaded with explosive and is a cruel and lethal weapon. The bowhead, or Greenland right whale, was one of the first species to be hunted to commercial extinction. The blue whale, the largest animal ever to have lived (100 feet, over 100 tons), was ruthlessly hunted from 1910 to 1967. The 60ft sei whale has only been intensively hunted since the early 1960s with the collapse of the larger blue and fin whale stocks. Now the 30ft minke whale, one of the most recent to be exploited, is one of the most important species for the industry. Whales have been hunted for their oil, their meat, for ambergris (used in soaps and perfumes), for almost every part of their body. But now that substitutes are available, the all-out slaughter can and should stop. Only Japan and Russia are still prominent as whale-catchers.

1	Grenade	6	Canon
2	Barbs (after explosion)	7	Unpointed head prevents ricochets
3	Barbs (before explosion)	8	Head pivots downwards on oblique hits
4	Slotted shaft	9	Belt holds barbs in place
5	Sight	10	Whale line

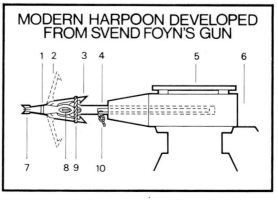

MODERN HARPOON DEVELOPED FROM SVEND FOYN'S GUN

Sei Whale

Blue Whale

Minke Whale

Bowhead Right Whale

13

THE SEAS MUST LIVE
by Robert Allen

The feeding, resting, breeding, and nursery areas of many marine animals are being damaged or destroyed. And many kinds of marine creatures— ranging from marine mammals through fish, seabirds, and countless smaller organisms—are themselves being over-exploited. The seas and oceans, and the life that lives in them, are a global commons and a global responsibility. Their survival is ultimately critical for the well-being of humanity. The World Wildlife Fund has therefore launched a major two-year Marine Campaign, based on a conservation program created by the International Union for Conservation of Nature and Natural Resources (IUCN). This article examines some important aspects of the campaign, and shows why it is vital for us all that 'The Seas Must Live'.

Critical habitats

Our daily bread may one day come from the sea—not just metaphorically, as much of our food does already—but literally. Scientists believe that eelgrass (*Zostera marina*), one of the few plants that grow and flower under the sea, is a potential food crop that could be cultivated in tropical shallows around the world. Flour from eelgrass grain is as nourishing as that from other grains and, like wheat flour, is bland and can be variously flavored.

So far the only known use of eelgrass as human food is by the Seri Indians on the Gulf of California. Traditionally, the Seri made a porridge out of it, mixed with sea turtle oil or honey. However, until more research is done, eelgrass and other seagrasses will remain of great but indirect importance to people. On the seas' meadows of flowering plants graze turtles, dugongs, manatees, and waterfowl. The best developed coral reefs occur primarily in association with dense seagrass meadows, and where seagrasses are sparse, coral reefs are relatively poor.

Seagrass meadows, along with beds of kelp and other seaweeds, and mangroves and salt-marshes, provide the nutritional beginnings of many of the world's most valuable fisheries. Collectively, they have been estimated to support two-thirds of the world's entire fish harvest. In the US alone, the final market value of fish that are dependent on or associated with estuaries has been put at $1.1 billion.

Seagrass meadows, seaweed beds, and coastal wetlands (mangroves, salt-marshes, lagoons, and so on) are known as critical marine habitats—critical for sea-dwellers, because they provide them with food and shelter; and critical for people, because of their fundamental role in the economies of the seas. Highly productive areas like coastal wetlands and offshore upwellings of nutrients; richly diverse communities of animals like coral reefs; and the feeding, breeding and resting areas of whales, seals, seabirds, and sea turtles—all are critical habitats. If too many are damaged or destroyed, then the harvest of the seas will diminish and eventually disappear.

Many critical marine habitats are already being wrecked. Reefs in Thailand are being dismembered of their finest shells and corals for sale to souvenir-hungry tourists. Sri Lanka's coral reefs are being quarried for building materials. Coastal wetlands the world over are being poisoned by pollution or obliterated by dredging and filling.

A global network of marine parks and reserves is essential for the protection of critical habitats, but its establishment faces two big obstacles. First, most nations continue to regard the sea as both a cornucopia and a waste disposal unit of limitless capacity, and are reluctant to set aside areas for apparently non-economic purposes. Yet without such protected areas the cornucopia cannot cope and the waste disposal unit will waste away.

Second, the seas and their creatures have no respect for national sovereignty, but potential marine parks are often within the territorial waters of more than one country—for example,

Unlike the other great whales, the sperm whale is toothed and feeds on giant squid and other large cephalopods, which it catches at great depths. It is exploited largely for its oil, which is used as a high-grade lubricant

Golfo de Fonseca (El Salvador, Honduras, and Nicaragua) and the Wadden Sea (Denmark, Germany, and the Netherlands). This demands an unusual degree of international co-operation. Even if one country sets up an adequate number of coastal and marine reserves, this will not be enough to save the life of the seas if other countries do not do the same. Many marine animals depend on a number of different habitats, often thousands of miles apart.

If the gray whales are to flourish, their calving lagoons in Mexico must be protected from industrial development and excessive disturbance by tourists, their feeding grounds in the Bering Sea must remain productive and available to them, and the route they travel between these areas must not be made intolerable for them by shipping and pleasure craft.

Many coastal waders migrate extraordinary distances—for example from the Arctic via western Europe to sub-Saharan Africa. Their flyways link numerous inland and coastal wetlands, most of them important and some essential as wintering, molting, or breeding grounds, or simply as staging posts on the long journeys north and south.

International systems of marine parks and reserves are vital—but not enough. Coral reefs, seagrass meadows, and coastal wetlands are not self-contained entities but parts of a continuum extending from the land to the open ocean, and from one part of the ocean to another. The oceans have their boundaries, but they are subtle and do not always correspond with our popular conceptions of them. Currents, upwellings, and salinity and temperature differences can act as barriers. The coast, by contrast, often unites rather than separates land and sea.

As highlands dissolve into the oceans, the streams and rivers of the world carry in suspension enormous cargoes of minerals, much of which, when the rivers grow sluggish, they deposit at their mouths. These mineral deposits fertilize the salt marshes and mangroves on whose decaying vegetation birds, fish, and sea mammals ultimately feed. Careless manipulation of rivers can therefore reduce the productivity of the seas, as well as affect sensitive marine animals in other ways. Each spring, belugas (or white whales), which live in the seas off Canada, Alaska, Greenland, Norway, and the Soviet Union, enter estuaries with a warm water run-off to breed. If the water is restricted

by a dam, the belugas do not return.

Without intelligent, knowledgeable management both of river systems and of the open seas, reserves lose much of their reason for existence. For this reason, the IUCN/WWF marine conservation program has placed great emphasis on both. Nothing is static. The land and the sea are one. We need institutions and methods that recognize this—and a major aim of WWF's campaign 'The Seas Must Live' is to show that such institutions and methods are not an idle dream but a practical possibility.

In the Pacific: islanders and ocean are on the brink of a new harmony

White beaches, blue skies, a turquoise sea, and palm trees swaying in a warm breeze: that is the city-dweller's romantic vision of the coral atoll. The reality is quite different. For the atoll-dweller, atolls are deserts within a desert: scraps of infertile soil marooned in a saltwater waste. That the Polynesian and Micronesian peoples of the Pacific have been able to live and flourish on them is due principally to two crucial factors. First, the reef and sea area between the land and the open ocean is richly productive. And second, the islanders are born conservationists.

Cooking reef fish over a coconut husk fire on Satawal, one of the Caroline Islands of Micronesia (left). The peoples of Micronesia, and Polynesia, have managed to flourish on atolls partly because they are born conservationists

Bora Bora Island (above) in French Polynesia. Many Pacific islands and atolls have been radically transformed in recent years—but the islanders will need to retain their traditional conservation measures, though in modernized form, if their fragile ecology is not to be destroyed completely

Apart from growing breadfruit, bananas, and a few root-crops like taro, the inhabitants of atolls live almost as hunter-gatherers: hunting and gathering the produce of reef and sea, catching birds and collecting their eggs, and gathering the fruit of coconuts and pandanus. Over the centuries, many of the islanders have developed a close, balanced relationship with the animals of the sea on which they depend so heavily.

On Pukapuka atoll in the Cook Islands, great care is taken still to make sure that marine resources are not overexploited. Seabird nesting and resting areas, and the lagoon, reef, and adjoining sea are treated as reserves. No one may take crabs, fish, eggs, or seabirds from the reserves until the village leaders decide that stocks are large enough to be harvested safely. The adults in each village take turns at guard duty, and when a reserve area is periodically opened, all adults receive equal shares (and children equal part-shares).

This system guarantees a fair share for everyone, as well as ensuring that harvests are kept at a level that can be sustained. The system is typical of the Pacific way of life.

Or rather it was. Like the rest of the world, the Pacific has undergone a transformation in recent years, and only a few island communities retain their traditions as completely as do the Pukapukans. Although seabirds continue to be an important source of food, the old constraints on their use have declined, and so therefore have the numbers of birds. On Raroia, in the Tuamotu archipelago (French Polynesia), the Polynesian sandpiper, little rail, and fruit dove have been exterminated, and populations of boobies and sooty terns are very low.

Far to the west, on the remote Tokelau islands, traditional prohibitions have almost entirely lapsed, and any number of birds or eggs may be taken by anyone on his own family holding. Only on communal land do traditional regulations still apply. As a result, most of the birds sought for food (such as noddy terns) are steadily declining. Similarly, long-established fishing methods that did not damage the reefs or overexploit stocks are being replaced by poisoning, dynamiting, and other techniques bringing quick returns at first but eventually no returns at all.

The erosion of traditional conservation measures poses a real threat to atoll communi-

ties, since fish and seabirds are their only readily available sources of protein. Canned meat and fish are alternatives, but their purchase seriously strains the islanders' fragile economies. There can be no going back to the good old days, of course. The pressures of change are too great. But although the atoll-dwellers' ways of life are bound to alter, they will still need to conserve the resources of the sea, so absolute is their dependence on them. Traditional conservation practises have to be modernized, not abolished. And traditional knowledge has to be retained, not dismissed as old-fashioned nonsense.

It is ironic that the children of the islanders are being taught the superior wisdom of Western science at a time when many scientists are beginning to recognize the scientific validity of traditional knowledge. The Pukapukans, for example, are expert ecologists. They have long correlated the habits and movements of fish with the rising and setting of various stars. The Society Islanders knew what fish were around simply by looking at the birds. Mixed flocks of boobies and terns feeding eagerly with cries of excitement meant there were bonito that would take the hook and not run too fast. A few white terns circling rapidly indicated dolphins.

Traditional conservation knowledge and practises were fine under traditional social and economic circumstances. But throughout much of the Pacific they have proved incapable of withstanding the mounting pressures of commerce and population growth. It used to be thought that the only solution to such prob-

Palau is part of the US Trust Territory of the Pacific Islands. Its coral reefs are among the most spectacular in the world. But besides their beauty they are a vital part of the local fisheries, and they are now threatened by a wide-ranging plan to build a superport and petroleum store, with attendant industries

The sea otter, here eating a squid off Monterey, California, was once almost exterminated by the fur trade. But thanks to careful conservation measures its numbers have increased again to the point where some fishermen even view it as a competitor

lems was rapid industrialization. But few islanders relish the prospect of being imitation Europeans or Americans any more than they cling nostalgically to the ways of their grandparents. What many of them would like—and what is clearly needed—is a bit of both: to enjoy some of the good things of an urban economy, while retaining certain qualities of their own culture.

Fortunately, development theory is beginning to swing their way. The basis of the relatively new concept of ecodevelopment is that development of a locality should take the fullest sustainable advantage of that locality's physical, biological, and cultural resources. This means, for example, that schools should be provided with teachers and textbooks which reinforce traditional understanding of the environment—instead of undermining it on the grounds that it is not 'scientific'. It means that new legislation should buttress local control of resource use rather than sweep it away. And it means the introduction of technologies (often quite simple ones, such as more seaworthy boats) to help people make use of resources they have hitherto scarcely harvested, like the tuna of the open sea.

The Pacific is pre-eminently the ocean of atolls—with three times as many as all the other oceans put together. The Pacific's atoll-dwellers have learned once already to live in rare harmony with their remarkable ocean universe. The hope is that with a bit of help from their friends they will learn to do so again.

Pollution: one drop in the ocean too many

Ask a sea duck or a sea otter if pollution should be stopped and it might not say yes. Because although most pollution is bad, some is good. The elegant city of Edinburgh in Scotland burdens her coastal waters with more than 53 million gallons of sewage a day. Extensive mussel beds have grown around the city's sewage outfalls. The shellfish are of course quite unfit for humans to eat, but the sea ducks love them. Some 30,000 scaup, several thousand eiders, and many other seabirds flock to Edinburgh for its year-long festival of filthy food.

They that go down to the sea in ships and throw their empty beer-cans over the side are not regarded as social menaces by California's sea otters. Octopuses, no lovers of wide open spaces, have discovered that aluminium cans make ideal homes. And sea otters, great lovers of octopuses, have discovered that discarded cans are not necessarily empty. If they see a can they rip it open and eat the occupant.

Yet for sea ducks and sea otters other forms of pollution are a serious threat. Oil slicks at sea, because of their peculiar optical properties, appear to birds to look remarkably like shoals of fish. This is the most likely explanation of why the long-tailed duck actually prefers to settle on oil patches—with disastrous results. Oil imperils the otter, too. If soiled, sea otter fur loses its insulating property, and the animal dies.

Pollution of various kinds makes life miserable — and sometimes impossible — for many sea-dwellers. Refinery effluents kill salt-marsh vegetation, and even very low concentrations of copper and zinc in estuaries can deter salmon from running upstream to spawn. Ordinary organic wastes like sewage can disrupt fish feeding and nursery grounds in a number of ways. Oxygen can be so reduced that adults are forced out of the area, or eggs are either prevented from hatching or (if they hatch) the larvae are unable to develop. Food organisms may be replaced by organisms that are tolerant of pollution but which the fish do not eat. Or larval development can be hindered or stopped altogether if there are growths of injurious bacteria or an excessive increase in turbidity.

Turbidity is a serious threat to coral reefs, and one that is growing. The most extreme form of turbidity is sedimentation—the deposition of silt carried down by rivers and streams. Corals have long had to contend with this, and they can rid themselves of normal amounts of falling sediment. But reckless forestry, farming, and ranching have greatly increased erosion and the loads carried to the sea.

Millions of tons of valuable soil are deposited in lagoons in the Virgin Islands, Hawaii, Australia, Tanzania, and elsewhere, killing the corals and destroying entire reef communities. Dumping and dredging also cause irreparable damage. Large-scale dredging in French Polynesia, for example, by raising clouds of fine sediment for long periods, has already destroyed important sections of reefs.

Coral reefs, like many other sensitive coastal environments, increasingly suffer from sewage pollution. The best known example is Kaneohe Bay, in the Hawaiian island of Oahu. Described half a century ago as 'one of the most favourable localities' for coral growth, more than 99 per cent of the corals at the south end of the bay are now dead—killed by the nearly 400,000 cubic feet of sewage that enter the bay every day.

More local, but generally even more devastating than sewage, is waste heat pollution. Many coral species die if exposed for up to twenty-four hours to a temperature only 5 to 6°C higher than normal. Prolonged temperature increases of only 3°C kill these corals in the end. Not surprisingly then, waste heat from power stations has devastated a number of reefs, especially in Florida.

The ruinous effects on corals of quite commonplace pollution explains the alarm of ecologists over the proposed superport in Palau, part of the US Trust Territory of the Pacific Islands. Palau's coral reefs are among the most pristine and spectacular in the Pacific. Quite apart from their stunning beauty, the reefs are a vital part of the local fisheries and are central to the livelihood of the Palauans. If the proposal to build a superport and petroleum store (not to mention the proposed construction of a major refinery, petrochemical plant and associated industries) were to go ahead, the productivity of Palau's reefs and lagoons could plummet.

Accordingly, the IUCN is to undertake an independent study of the ecological and economic opportunities available to the Palauans if the superport is rejected, compared with those available if it is built. The study is part of the joint IUCN/WWF Marine Program, and one of a number of efforts being carried out by environmental and public interest groups in Palau and the United States.

The people of Palau face a critical choice—as indeed do all the peoples of the world: to live with the sea or against it. They are being forced to make that choice before the rest of the world has begun even to realize that the choice exists. Which of course, in the end, it doesn't.

Trade in corals, crocs and turtles: luxuries the tropical poor cannot afford

The time between a coastal crocodile's birth and the day he meets his handbag-maker is short and getting shorter. The skin of the estuarine (or saltwater) crocodile provides leather of the highest quality, and many of them are shot even before they have a chance to breed.

Crocodiles are not cuddly creatures, and their skin looks good on human beings. So the live-crocodile lobby is reduced to a tiny coterie of eccentrics, heavily outgunned by the leather-goods industry and everybody else convinced that the only good crocodile is a dead one. All that stands between most crocodiles (coastal and freshwater) and extinction is an international agreement controlling trade in endangered wild animals and plants: the Convention on International Trade in Endangered Species of Wild Fauna and Flora.

Crocodiles and alligators are now so threatened that all species have had to be listed in the convention, which prohibits international trade in some, and requires trade in others to be carefully monitored. Among the latter are the two coastal species, the American crocodile and the estuarine crocodile.

International trade is making heavy inroads on the populations of a great many marine animals. Every year, the Philippines exports from two to three and a half million tropical marine fish for aquaria. In 1974, Singapore imported more than thirty-nine million aquarium fish. In the same year, Tanzania exported nearly three hundred tons of corals and shells.

Colorful fish, corals, and shells look nice in the home, but the quantities being torn from their native habitats could be devastating for the health of coral reefs and other tropical sea environments. As part of the Marine Program, the trade control group of IUCN will in-

This Australian estuarine crocodile (right), like others of its tribe, has the dual misfortune of an evil reputation combined with a hide that is much coveted for shoes, belts, and so forth. Over-exploitation is responsible for much of the decline in animal populations—and the tempting display of shells at Bangkok's 'Sunday Market' (below right) is typical of thousands of similar displays around the Indo-Pacific oceans

sought after by local collectors.

The ivory trade is another threat to marine animals. Small boatloads of walrus heads have been observed in Alaska, the animals decapitated for their valuable tusks. Even the not uncommon practise of making some 'walrus' ivory carvings out of the ivory of African elephants has not prevented the rise in walrus killing. Any animal unfortunate enough to possess big teeth is on the hit list of the trinket trade.

For these and other marine animals hope lies in the endangered species convention. This prohibits international trade only in those species that otherwise would be unlikely to survive. Less threatened animals can be traded, but the trade is monitored so that if it does grow to dangerous levels, the species concerned can be transferred to the tougher section of the convention.

Much trade in marine life—in aquarium fish, corals and shells, in crocodile skins and in turtle products—is for the luxury markets of industrial countries. Some of it could continue if levels were reduced. But current levels are so high that they threaten to destroy not just the luxury markets but the very livelihoods of a great many of the tropical poor.

San Francisco: a link in the chain of marine life

San Francisco, scene of the launch of World Wildlife Fund's marine program, is washed by the California Current, the home and highway of twenty-eight species of whales, six species of seals, and the sea otter. By their travels, these animals link San Francisco with the rest of the Pacific—and with the rest of the world. Although nations continue to partition the seas amongst themselves, the life of the seas unites them still.

Follow the gray whales. Twice a year, the huge creatures pass San Francisco to and from their calving grounds in the lagoons of Mexico and their feeding grounds in the Bering Sea—each bearing its cargo of invertebrate associates, each a planet of life in the ocean universe. In the southern part of the gray whale's range, dolphins move in and out of the Channel Islands, voyaging into the open ocean twice a year: northwest in July, south in December. The Channel Islands are also the starting point of the California sea lion's migration, following the gray whale route north as far as Vancouver

vestigate the trade in fish, corals, and shells, focusing on key hotspots such as Thailand, Hong Kong, Malaysia, the Philippines, Japan, and Hawaii. One purpose of the investigation is to find out what areas are under the greatest pressure, and what precisely are the effects of the trade, particularly on coral reefs.

Some molluscs are believed to be threatened already. The Government of Mauritius is worried about the status of the imperial harp shell and also of two species of cowrie, one found only in Mauritius and the other confined to Mauritius and the Island of Reunion. All three are rare and beautiful, bringing high prices from shell dealers and thus eagerly

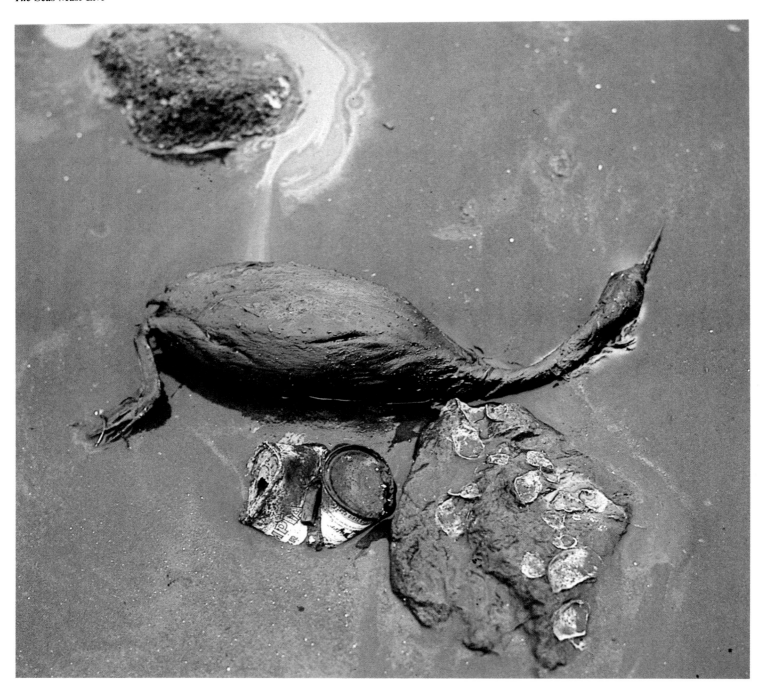

Oil is one of the more easily visible pollutants of the seas, especially the important surface layers. Oil pollution, whether from tanker spills, offshore wells, or the illegal washing of tanks at sea, is responsible for killing many wild animals every year. The western grebe (above) has fallen victim to an oil spill near San Francisco. Also in San Francisco (left), the sign underlines the fact that the water flowing beneath the Golden Gate bridge may be a lot less inviting than the name suggests

Like all whales the beluga (near right), or white whale, is threatened by excessive hunting, though it is not part of a major industry like the large oceanic whales

That long-distance champion, the Arctic tern (far right) sums up the interdependence of all marine life; it migrates annually from Arctic to Antarctic, enjoying summer all the way

Island.

The gray whale families have farther to go though—right to the Bering Sea, the sea that binds the two super-powers of the globe, the Soviet Union and the United States. The Bering Sea is home to 271 million birds— 14,500 tons of them. One of the bird species that depends on the hospitality of its shores is the bristle-thighed curlew, which breeds in Alaska and winters in the South Pacific. From the coastal waters of the Bering Sea, the bristle-thighed curlew gets the energy it needs for one of the most remarkable of all migrations: 2500 miles in a single soaring hop to Hawaii, the first of the bird's staging posts on its way to the islands of the tropical south—Samoa, the Cook Islands, Tahiti . . .

The Cook Islands are worth going to. One of them is Manuae, a tiny coral atoll that has made history three times: it was the first of the Cooks to have been discovered by the Polynesians who live there today; the first of the Cooks to have been sighted by Captain James Cook, whose name the islands still bear; and it is the first world marine park—given to 'world science and for the benefit of mankind' by the Cook Islanders and their government. Truly, a generous, imaginative challenge to the nations of the world to seek marine policies that will benefit all peoples, present and to come.

Marine animals link San Francisco not only with the Bering Sea and thence with the South Pacific, but also with Japan. Albacore are known to migrate between the offshore waters of Japan and those of southern California. And from waters not far from Japan, we may follow sperm whales to Indonesia and the Indian Ocean, where humpback whales take us down the east coast of Africa to the Southern Ocean.

The Southern Ocean is the least exploited of all the oceans. Defined as the area between the shore-fast ice of Antarctica and the Antarctic Convergence (the narrow zone where cold waters flowing north meet warm waters flowing south), the Southern Ocean is also the only ocean to which few if any nations have any valid claim. But the carve-up is beginning. Soviet and Japanese fleets have already begun fishing for krill, the tiny shrimp-like animals that swarm in the cold waters in enormous quantities, and are said to be the world's largest source of untapped protein.

Well, not entirely untapped. Krill are the major food of five species of large whales, including the endangered blue whale and humpback whale, and are also important for three species of seals, many seabird species, and several species of fish. The whales, already reduced by over-hunting, could be despatched into oblivion once and for all if the industrial nations of the world snatch the krill from their mouths. The Southern Ocean confronts us with the choice of developing a civilized system of managing the seas, or of succumbing to a mad scramble to be first in a grand finale of oceanic pillage and rape.

Antarctica may seem far away from San Francisco, but the links are nevertheless there. To complete our westward progress with the hard-travelling life of the seas, we need only accompany the Arctic tern. This bird is a real daylight-saver, spending nightless winters in the Antarctic, and then (on one of its routes) proceeding gracefully up the west coast of South America, past California, to enjoy nightless summers in the Arctic.

The creatures of the seas go their wide-ranging ways, linking the peoples of different lands with each other. It is in the hands of all these peoples to ensure that the whales, seals, seabirds, sea turtles, and fish continue to have some place to go to.

MAMMALS

SAVING THE TIGER

by Peter Jackson

A large tiger lay dozing in a shady corner of the jungle, belly swollen with the previous night's meal, a great paw occasionally brushing a fly from his face. He was a picture of contentment and complete relaxation. And yet only a few yards away I was sitting with some friends on an elephant watching him. We deliberately coughed and he opened sleepy eyes once or twice, but after that he could not be bothered whatever noise we made.

To see so relaxed and confident a representative of a species which has been brought near to extinction by persistent trophy hunting, while its habitat has been largely destroyed, is a heart-warming experience for a conservationist. The incident took place in the Kanha Tiger Reserve in central India, and is a tribute to the effectiveness of the protection provided by one of the most comprehensive schemes for saving an endangered species that has so far been launched—Project Tiger.

The Indian project is one of the principal parts of an overall campaign which was launched by the World Wildlife Fund under the title 'Operation Tiger' when it was apparent that without urgent action the tiger was doomed to extinction in the very near future.

The alarm was sounded at the General Assembly of the International Union for Conservation of Nature and Natural Resources (IUCN) in Delhi in 1969. Until then there were still references in many quarters to tigers being abundant. But in Delhi the distinguished gathering of scientists and conservationists were told the blunt truth—there remained only about 2500 tigers in India, while most of the other seven sub-species were in a far more parlous state. Yet the tiger was still considered fair game and its skin was becoming a desired ornament for homes in wealthy countries.

Farmers and other local people, encouraged by traders, used poisonous pesticides planted in tiger kills to collect skins which would bring them cash equal to their normal income for a whole year or more. Despite the experts' proclaimed concern it still took time to convince some authorities in areas where tigers were still in reasonable numbers that there was a serious danger. Thus it was not until more than two years later that a complete ban on killing tigers was in force throughout India. Meanwhile, under the dynamic leadership of one of its international trustees, Guy Mountfort, the World Wildlife Fund prepared its then greatest-ever fund-raising drive—a million dollars for Operation Tiger. It was launched in September 1972 with the declaration:

The tiger is one of the most impressive and beautiful wild animals in the world. Its survival is threatened because mankind has destroyed its home and hunted it mercilessly. Surely none of us wish to see this wonderful creature wiped out. But wiped out it will be unless strenuous efforts are made now.

In India a tiger census found traces of only 1800 tigers thoughout this vast land where there had been probably 40,000 only four decades earlier. Not more than 200 tigers were (generously) estimated to survive in adjoining Nepal, where the Terai, the area running along

The Siberian tiger is the largest of the races of the tiger, and though much reduced in number in the wild, it is well protected and has a good chance of survival

the foot of the Himalayas, had once been a vast natural sanctuary for wildlife, protected from human intrusion by virulent strains of malaria. The advent of DDT led to the conquest of malaria and settlement of the Terai, both in Nepal and India, during the 1950s and 1960s. The wild habitat was rapidly converted to agriculture, and all forms of wildlife were mercilessly slaughtered. It was disastrous for the tiger, faced with loss of its habitat and prey species, while being hunted at the same time.

In Bangladesh tigers had a measure of protection because of their semi-aquatic life-style in the Sunderbans, the extensive mangrove jungles of the delta fringing the Bay of Bengal, where there is little human habitation.

The Indian sub-continent is perhaps associated with the tiger more than any other area. But in fact the tiger in its heyday was found from the Caspian to the Pacific, and from Siberia to Indonesia. Taxonomists identified eight forms:

Panthera tigris tigris, the Bengal, or Indian tiger, with males averaging about nine feet and weighing nearly 440 pounds.

P.t. virgata, the Caspian tiger, tending to be smaller with a thick winter coat, dark, with close-set stripes. It lived in Iran, Turkey, Iraq, and what is now Soviet Central Asia.

P.t. altaica, the Siberian tiger, more powerfully built than other races and lighter in color. It ranged the Amur River basin in the Far East, Northeast China, and Korea.

P.t. sondaica, the Javan tiger, small and dark, with stripes sometimes degenerating into spots.

P.t. amoyensis, the Chinese tiger, much smaller than the Siberian, more richly colored and more heavily striped.

P.t. balica, the Bali tiger, smallest of the sub-species, with short close fur.

P.t. sumatrae, the Sumatran tiger, smaller than the Indian tiger and more fully striped and showing less white.

P.t. corbetti, the Indo-Chinese tiger, smaller and darker than the Indian tiger with more numerous, rather short, narrow, and rarely-doubled stripes. It ranges from Burma through continental South-East Asia to Vietnam.

There has been no sign of the Bali tiger for several years, and it is feared extinct. Far to the

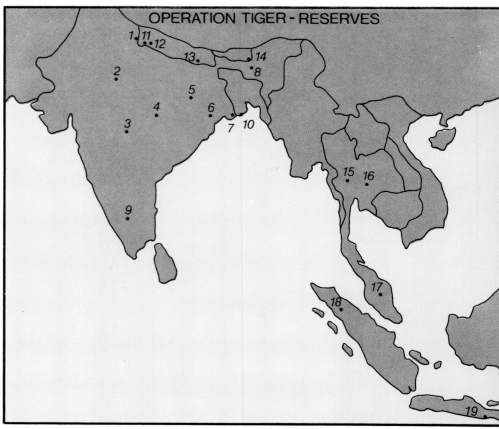

OPERATION TIGER - RESERVES

Experts warily track a tiger whose trail is easily seen in the soft sand (left). The pregnant tigress (right) has caught her foot in a savage-looking trap, and is struggling to free herself. Soon after this photograph was taken she disappeared completely, together with the trap, and it was thought that poachers had taken her. But months later she was seen alive, and hardly the worse for wear. Apparently she had managed to get the trap off her foot

west the Caspian tiger appears to be nearly gone. Soviet scientists say there are no more in their territory, while searches in Iran have failed to produce any trace. Some skins which came on the market in Turkey in recent years gave hope, however, that in the southeast of that country and in neighboring areas of Iraq there might be a small relict population.

On the heavily populated island of Java the tiger just survives in the extreme east, where signs of four or five have been found. Although an extensive reserve has been set aside at Meru Betiri the Javan tiger is clearly on the verge of extinction.

Moving to the neighboring island of Sumatra, there is a slightly better situation. A World Wildlife Fund survey in 1975 produced an estimate of about 800 Sumatran tigers. But despite legal protection they are being killed at the rate of about 100 a year, and unless this can be stopped they must be doomed.

Soviet authorities say that the Siberian tiger is safe, with about 120 or so in reserves north of Vladivostok. Some are believed still to survive in the north of Korea and in China.

Virtually nothing is known of the Chinese tiger. Until a few years ago it was still con-sidered a pest to be destroyed, but the Chinese Government now says that it is fully protected, as is the Indo-Chinese tiger found in the extreme south of the country.

In fact, the Indo-Chinese tiger is the only sub-species, apart from the Indian, still existing in reasonable numbers, even if scattered through a large area where the forests are rapidly being destroyed. Legal protection is given in Malaysia and Thailand.

Although tiger conservation projects are under way in Java and Thailand, Project Tiger in India is undoubtedly the most comprehensive scheme. It was launched in 1973 with the full backing of the Prime Minister, Mrs Indira Gandhi, who put one of her senior Cabinet colleagues, Dr Karan Singh, in charge. The six-year program concentrates on nine special reserves, which cover most of the main examples of tiger habitat, including dry thorn forest at Ranthambhor (Rajasthan), mangrove swamps in the Sunderbans in Bengal, and various other types of forest at Palamau (Bihar), Simlipal (Orissa), Corbett (Uttar Pradesh), Bandipur (Karnataka), Kanha (Madhya Pradesh), Melghat (Maharashtra), and Manas (Assam), which is linked to the adjoining mountain area

in Bhutan.

All these areas were in fact reserves of some kind, but forestry operations were still going on. Under Project Tiger the reserves now have core areas reserved strictly for the tiger. Disturbance is kept to the minimum and human activity is restricted to necessary scientific and conservation measures. Detailed management plans have been put into operation, and monitoring of vegetation and animal populations is being initiated. Technical advice, if required, is being made available by the World Wildlife Fund and the IUCN.

Equipment has been an important requirement. Jeeps, pick-up trucks, jet speedboats for patrolling the delta region of the Sunderbans, and camels for the arid, sandy region of Ranthambhor have been provided. The World Wildlife Fund has also helped with office and administrative equipment, and is supplying speciality books and other publications for the project headquarters and the tiger reserves. Radio networks have also been provided.

One of the greatest achievements has been the successful removal of villages from the Kanha and Ranthambhor reserves. The people have been comfortably settled on good land with new houses and communal facilities. The wild animals quickly reoccupied the forsaken agricultural land, which will again become part of the jungle.

Fire has been an annual scourge of the Indian forests in the dry seasons. Often the fires were the result of carelessness, of failure to extinguish camp fires, or throwing away lighted cigarette ends. But some were deliberately started in order to flush game for hunting, or to kill trees which could then legitimately be claimed for firewood. Now, fire-control measures are in force, including the clearing of fire breaks and controlled burning of the timber-like leaf litter. Watch-towers have been built and radio networks link them with reserve headquarters.

Fire-fighting teams can move quickly, and as a result the Project Tiger authorities were able to report that in Kanha, for example, no serious fires occurred during the 1976 dry season—'Kanha has been saved', to quote the report to the World Wildlife Fund.

The radio networks also help the endless battle against poachers. While it would be

Indian or Bengal tigers: in
Kanha National Park (left),
and cooling off (right)

foolish to suggest that tiger poaching has been entirely eliminated, it seems clear that the combination of reinforced protection, and the vigilance of the police and customs authorities has reduced it considerably. Import bans in the United States and Britain have helped to check demand. Nevertheless, contraband stocks of skins of tiger, leopard, and other endangered species have been uncovered, and it seems all too likely that diplomatic immunity has been and is being used to smuggle out wildlife products.

While there is reason to feel happy about the progress in the tiger reserves, it has to be admitted that they are in most cases much smaller than desirable. Few of them can hold more than 40 or 50 tigers, and although most have a buffer zone in which some more animals live, there is no way in which tigers can move from one reserve to another. It is unlikely that any area contains the 300 tigers able to interbreed, which is suggested by geneticists as necessary to maintain the character of the animal. The tiger reserves are in fact like islands in an ocean of humanity.

Fewer than 400 tigers are in the special sanctuaries, leaving over three times that number in a hundred or so other reserves. They have legal protection, but forestry operations continue in their territories, and thus they are disturbed and vulnerable to poaching. However, it cannot be expected that a densely populated country like India should leave valuable forest resources completely untouched.

Among the reserves outside the scope of Project Tiger special mention must be made of Dudhwa, near the southwestern tip of Nepal, which has now been made the core area of the North Kheri National Park. Only a ceaseless battle by a militant farmer-conservationist, Kunwar Arjan Singh, has saved the tiger and other wild animals there—including the largest surviving herd of the threatened swamp deer. In many other areas there was no champion to defend the lord of the jungle and he vanished. The tiger is not by nature a man-killer or man-eater, and throughout the ages tigers and men have co-existed. True there are occasions when a surprised or frightened tiger lashes out and kills people, but often these incidents are rather like the result of wandering carelessly in a city and getting run over by a car or bus. Still,

29

This historic photo of a dead Bali tiger (above) was taken in 1935. This race of tiger is now almost certainly extinct

Dr Karan Singh (left), Chairman of Project Tiger, using the radio telephone supplied by World Wildlife India

some tigers do become habitual man-eaters, usually through incapacity to hunt normally because of age or injury. In such cases there is no alternative to killing them. However, a stray case of man-killing may not warrant such action and in fact two tigers responsible recently for human deaths have been trapped and put into zoos.

In Nepal considerable progress has also been made in conserving the tiger. Here three reserves are involved. The largest and most important is the Royal Chitawan National Park on the Rapti river southwest of Kathmandu, which also holds more than 200 great Indian rhinoceroses, the second largest surviving population after Kaziranga in India.

Chitawan has been the scene of a study of tiger ecology carried out with World Wildlife Fund aid under the auspices of the Smithsonian Institution. Tigers and leopards have been tranquillized and fitted with radio collars so that their movements can be tracked. The studies have shown how close to villages and human activity the big cats may go about their lives.

Research of this kind is not without hazards. Kirti Man Tamang, the Principal Investigator, was chased up a tree by a tigress he was watching. The tigress lunged at him, lacerating his flesh and making him fall. Curiously the tigress, which had cubs nearby, did not press her attack, but lay and observed Kirti until his companions on an elephant rescued him. Kirti recovered in hospital and returned to watch his tigers.

Nepal has two other reserves with tiger at Karnali and Sukhla Phanta in the southwest. They harbor about 30 tigers each, and Sukhla Phanta also has a healthy population of swamp deer.

Thailand began a serious tiger conservation project in 1976 with the establishment of sanctuaries at Huay Kha Khaeng, Tung Yai, and Salek Pra in the Kwae Yai River basin in the west of the country. At the same time the important Khao Yai National Park, northeast of Bangkok, also holds an important tiger population. As with India the World Wildlife Fund is helping with the provision of vehicles, radios, and other equipment to improve the protection and management of the areas.

Concern must be felt most of all about the tiger in Indonesia. Only the faintest hope remains that the Bali tiger might survive, but if so it could only be in such small numbers as to offer little hope for the future. The Javan tiger is right on the brink of extinction. A recent survey found evidence of only four or five, which are living in the Sukomade Kali in Meru Betiri in eastern Java. Unfortunately, this is an area with relatively few suitable prey species, while both leopard and wild dog compete for them with the tiger. Further surveys are underway as well as preparation of a conservation management plan for the area.

Despite the continued illegal killing of the Sumatran tiger, and economic development plans affecting its habitat, there is real hope that a suitable reserve can be established which will ensure its survival. The animal is already protected in the extensive Leuser Reserve, west of Medan, but another area is required as well and surveys are being carried out, together with negotiations with the Government and others who would be involved.

To sum up, it seems that the tiger now has a good chance of survival in India, Nepal, Thailand, Indonesia (Sumatra), and the USSR (Siberia). Real progress in conservation efforts has been made in India and Nepal, where the governments—with whom the ultimate responsibility must lie—are fully backing the conservationists.

The plight of the tiger is now well-known, and, what is of equal importance, it is seen as representative of the threat to wildlife in general. Saving the tiger can only be achieved by conserving its habitat with its full range of wildlife species, and the large natural areas involved are part of our natural heritage, which we have a duty to pass on to our successors.

ENDANGERED DEER

by Kenneth Whitehead

Of the forty living species of deer in the world, no fewer than seventeen are included in the *Red Data Book* of the IUCN as being endangered or vulnerable.

Many of the deer of northern India, Tibet, and China have been much reduced in numbers since the beginning of the century, and in almost every case the reasons have been the same—over-hunting and loss of habitat, the former undoubtedly made more effective by the accuracy of modern firearms. Unfortunately, information about the present status of some of the Asiatic deer is almost non-existent, and although lack of data may suggest near extinction, one always hopes that the picture is not as bad as might first appear.

Among the most endangered are the Yarkand deer (*Cervus elaphus yarkandensis*) of Chinese Turkestan and the shou (*Cervus elaphus wallichi*) of south-east Tibet and the adjacent valleys of Bhutan, and indeed the *Red Data Book* suggests that both might now be extinct. No recent information is available, either, concerning those other two deer of Tibet and western China, namely McNeill's deer (*Cervus canadensis macneilli*) and Thorold's or white-lipped deer (*Cervus albirostris*)—but at the beginning of World War II the population of the former was thought to be around 5000, while in 1964 Thorold's deer was already described as 'very rare and in need of special protection'.

The main reason for the decline in the wild of many of these Asiatic deer has been the merciless hunting by local people for the sake of their antlers, particularly while still in velvet. These are ground and dried to be used as an aphrodisiac. In recent years, however, it has been found possible to farm deer for the sole purpose of producing antlers which can be cut off

The pampas deer is one of four South American deer causing concern. This is the Brazilian subspecies of pampas deer, about which little is known, though it is not thought to be facing immediate danger of extinction

without the owner having to be killed—an operation that cannot, of course, be done with wild deer. According to a recent article in *China Pictorial*, Thorold's deer are now being domesticated on a farm in Chinghai (Tsinghai) Province, so the main cause of their decline may now be their salvation as domesticated stocks build up on the deer farms.

Rather more hopeful is the present status of both the Kashmir deer or hangul (*Cervus elaphus hanglu*) and the Bactrian or Bukharian deer (*Cervus elaphus bactrianus*), of northern Afghanistan and adjacent parts of Russian Turkestan. Throughout the range of the hangul in Kashmir and the Bactrian deer in Turkestan, hunting is totally prohibited, and although some poaching does occur, their numbers do seem to be slowly building up. A fairly recent report suggests that the population of these species would appear to be around 900 each. In northern Afghanistan, too, despite lack of any legal protection, the deer is just about holding its own, and a 1974 estimate suggested that the population there might be around 150 to 200.

Other Asiatic members of the genus *Cervus* whose status is causing concern are the swamp deer (*Cervus duvauceli*) of India, the thamin or brow-antlered deer (*Cervus eldi*) of Manipur and Thailand, and some of the sika deer races (*Cervus nippon*) of China and Japan.

Of the two subspecies of swamp deer, though the population of the northern race (*C. d. duvauceli*), which occurs principally in Uttar Pradesh, western Bengal, and Assam, is now estimated at about 4500 animals, it is doubtful if more than about 100 animals remain of the southern race (*C. d. branderi*), all of which are located in the Kanha National Park in Madhya Pradesh.

Forty years ago the population of swamp deer in the Kanha area was estimated at around 3000. Poaching and intrusion into its habitat by domestic stock seem to have been the principle causes of decline. The favorite habitat of the southern race is a large, grassy plain on which the deer can graze and rest. This is in sharp contrast to the northern race which is a dweller of swamp lands.

Another deer of southern Asia which is becoming scarce is the thamin or Eld's deer—sometimes called the brow-antlered deer—*Cervus eldi*. Three subspecies are recognized: *Cervus eldi eldi* from Manipur, *C. e. thamin*

from Burma, Tenasserim, and adjacent parts of Thailand, and *C. e. siamensis* from Thailand, whose range also extends into Vietnam and Hainan Island. Little is known about the present status of these races, but it seems probable that all are now extremely rare. About twelve years ago the late E. P. Gee, after discussing the situation of *C. e. eldi* with local forest officers and villagers, came to the conclusion that there were probably about 100 brow-antlered deer in the ten-square-mile sanctuary of Logtak Lake, Manipur. Much of the terrain in the Manipur Valley is a huge swamp over which the deer are able to walk on the floating reeds and grass, known locally as *phum* or *phumdi*. In Burma, before the introduction of guns, the thamin was extremely numerous, but it is doubtful if the total population now exceeds 4000 animals, the majority of which are to be found in the Shwebo, Meiktila, and Minbu forest divisions.

The plight of the Thailand brow-antlered deer (*C. e. siamensis*) is a little obscure, but in Thailand itself it is believed that only a few herds now remain at Nang Kong in the northeast and at Chieng Karn in the north. In the Khmer Republic (Cambodia), where it was at one time relatively common, the deer suffered heavy losses as the result of the war; since then, however, several reserves have been established and all hunting prohibited, but how successful these measures will be remains to be seen. So far as the deer on Hainan Island are concerned—locally referred to as *Po lu* (hillside deer) or *mei hua lu* (plum blossom deer)—a report published by the Zoological Research Laboratory of the Kwangtung Entomological Research suggested that although the deer was found 'in different parts of nine counties . . . the provisional estimate must be that the total population is small'.

One of the most beautiful antlered deer of Thailand—and indeed of the world—is Schomburgk's deer (*Cervus schomburgki*), but alas, it probably became extinct during the early 1930s, for the last recorded specimen was a stag killed by an officer of the Siamese police in 1931. Its last stronghold seems to have been in the great swampy plains around Paknam Po (Nakhon Sawan) in central Thailand, and possibly also in the Muang Petchabun area.

The sika deer (*Cervus nippon*) has a wide distribution in eastern Asia, and although some thirteen different races are recognized, many

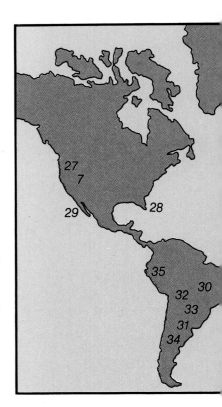

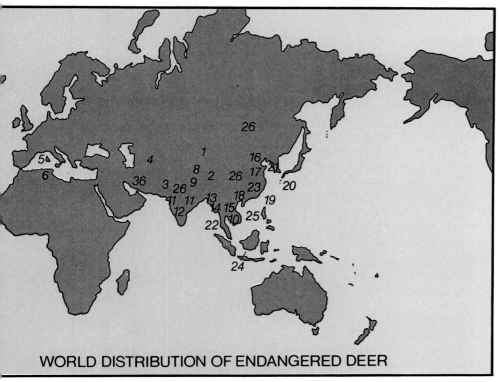

WORLD DISTRIBUTION OF ENDANGERED DEER

	Common name	Scientific name	Principal locality
1	Yarkand deer	Cervus elaphus yarkandensis	Chinese Turkestan
2	Shou	C.e. wallichi	Tibet
3	Kashmir deer	C.e. hanglu	Kashmir
4	Bactrian deer	C.e. bactrianus	Northern Afghanistan and Russian Turkestan
5	Corsican red deer	C.e. corsicanus	Corsica and Sardinia
6	Barbary deer	C.e. barbarus	Algeria and Tunisia
7	Tule elk (wapiti)	Cervus canadensis nannodes	California, USA
8	McNeill's deer	C.c. macneilli	Western China and Tibet
9	White-lipped deer	Cervus albirostris	Tibet
10	Schomburgk's deer	Cervus schomburgki	Thailand (extinct?)
11	Swamp deer	Cervus duvauceli duvauceli	North of Ganges, Assam, India
12	Swamp deer	C.d. branderi	North-central India
13	Eld's deer	Cervus eldi eldi	Manipur
14	Eld's deer	C.e. thamin	Burma, Tenasserim
15	Eld's deer	C.e. Siamensis	Thailand, Vietnam, Hainan Island
16	North China sika deer	Cervus nippon mandarinus	North China
17	Shansi sika deer	C.n. grassianus	Shansi, China
18	South China or Kopsch's deer	C.n. kopschi	South-east China
19	Formosan sika deer	C.n. taiouanus	Taiwan
20	Kerama sika deer	C.n. keramae	Middle Ryukyu Islands
21	Black muntjac	Muntiacus crinifrons	Eastern China
22	Fea's muntjac	M. feae	Tenasserim and Thailand
23	Tufted deer	Elaphodus cephalophus michianus	South-east China
24	Bawean deer	Axis kuhlii	Bawean Island
25	Calamian deer	Axis calamianensis	Calamian Islands
26	Musk deer	Moschus moschiferus (3 species)	Northern India and eastern Asia
27	Columbian white-tailed deer	Odocoileus virginianus leucurus	Oregon, USA
28	Key white-tailed deer	O.v. clavium	Florida Keys, USA
29	Cerros Island mule deer	O. hemionus cerrosensis	Cerros Island
30	Pampas deer	Ozotocerus bezoarticus bezoarticus	Brazil
31	Pampas deer	Ozotoceros bezoarticus celer	Argentina
32	Pampas deer	O.b. leucogaster	Central South America
33	Marsh deer	Blastocerus dichotomus	Central Brazil to north Argentina
34	Huemul	Hippocamelus bisulcus	Andes of Chile and Argentina
35	Huemul	H. antisensis	Northern Andes
36	Mesopotamian fallow deer	Dama dama mesopotamica	Iran (south)

of these, and in particular those present in China, are now considered endangered species. These include *C. n. mandarinus* of north China, *C. n. grassianus* of the Shansi district of central China, and *C. n. kopschi* of south-east China. Formerly the north China sika deer ranged over much of north-east China and in particular in the Shantung province, but from recent reports it would appear that it may now be extinct in a wild state. The Shansi sika is also facing extinction in the wild state, and although the status of the south China or Kopsch's Sika deer appears to be slightly better, it is, nevertheless, an endangered species.

The principle reason for the decline in population of these Chinese sika deer is hunting for antlers which are used in the preparation of an aphrodisiac. Fortunately, as already mentioned in the case of the white-lipped or Thorold's deer, many of the Chinese and Manchurian sika deer are now being farmed, with a result that antlers can be obtained from the living animal. This form of deer farming has undoubtedly, therefore, saved many of these Asiatic deer from extinction but it cannot repair the damage done to their habitat by local farmers who are turning the land over to cultivation, thus drastically reducing their range.

On the island of Taiwan (Formosa) there is an insular race of sika deer—the Formosan sika (*C. n. taiouanus*)—which, like some of the mainland forms, is now on the verge of extinction. During the years the island was under Japanese rule the deer were protected, but this is no longer the case. The deer have declined to near extinction and any that now remain in the wild state do so in the mountainous southern parts of the island. This deer is now kept in many zoos and parks throughout the world; while off the Chinese coast a number of Formosan sika are raised on Lu-tao (Green Island) for their antlers, a pair of which was said to be worth about $100 in 1972.

The kerama or Ryukyu sika (*C. n. keramae*) is found only on some of the uninhabited islands of the Ryukyu group, principal among which is the island of Yakabi where, in 1964, only about thirty animals remained as compared to 160 some ten years previously. This deer is prone to melanism, and occasionally all black animals occur. The status of the other five races of Japanese sika cause no concern.

Of the five species of muntjac, two are considered endangered—namely the black or hairy-fronted muntjac (*Muntiacus crinifrons*) of eastern China and Fea's muntjac (*M. feae*) of Tenasserim and Thailand. Very little is known about the status of the black muntjac and until recently only about three specimens appear to have been recorded—and two of these were taken some ninety years ago from Ningpo, Chekiang. It has always been assumed that the absence of sightings may have been due to the secretive nature of the animal—an assumption which is partially confirmed by a record in the zoological magazine of Anhui University Biology Department, which reports that between winter 1973 and spring 1974 eighty skins of the black muntjac were collected in the province of Anhui (Anhwei), which lies adjacent to Chekiang. It would appear, therefore, that this deer may not be as scarce as is generally assumed—indeed it may be quite plentiful in Anhui, for the report goes on to say that local hunting and animal husbandry departments consider this an animal that has to be controlled. Fea's muntjac may be more scarce, but in Thailand a recent report (1972) suggests that in some of the more remote mountainous areas 'it is not particularly scarce'. The flesh of both animals is much sought after and sold in the rural markets.

Little is known about the status of the tufted deer (*Elaphodus cephalophus*) which occurs in northern Burma and in central and southern China, but it would seem to be rare in much of its range. Three subspecies are recognized, and although the above quoted zoological magazine of Anhui University records that between the winter of 1973 and spring of 1974 twenty specimens of tufted deer were collected in the province of Anhui, it concludes by saying that this deer should be given the protection necessary for a precious animal that has a docile temperament, is easy to domesticate, and is one that has very good prospects for captive breeding.

Another Asiatic deer that is, at present, on the endangered list is the Bawean or Kuhl's deer (*Axis kuhlii*) which is confined to the island of Bawean situated to the north of Java. The most recent estimate (1969) suggests that there may be about 500 animals on the island, and although it is protected by law, this protection is not strictly enforced. Hunting by local fishermen, who are unable to put to sea during the early months of the year, is not considered as serious a threat as the clearing of forests to make way for increased cultivation, thus reducing the habitat area. Another possible threat to their survival, however, would appear to come from hunting by foreigners prospecting for off-shore oil deposits; if oil was to be found, the situation could deteriorate rapidly. A number of Bawean deer exist in Surabaja Zoo in Java.

A very similar deer to the Bawean deer is the Calamian deer (*Axis calamianensis*) which is restricted to the Calamian group of islands lying to the west of the main Philippine group, and in particular to the islands of Buswanga and Culion. Following a visit to the islands in February and March 1975, Major Ian Grimwood suggested that the total population of this deer on all the islands would not exceed more than about 900, with the biggest number, about 450, on Buswanga. 'The Calamian deer', he wrote,

has suffered a great reduction in numbers over the last thirty years and although nominally protected, it continues to decline in every part of its limited range . . . The species is unaffected by habitat destruction and the cause of its decline is solely illegal hunting. Unless that hunting can be brought under control, or an effective sanctuary can be created for it, the species therefore appears doomed to early extinction.

The Calamian deer is the only deer on the Calamian Islands and the sole representative of the genus *Axis* found anywhere in the Philippines, all the other deer being sambar (*Cervus unicolor*). The skull and antlers of the Calamian deer, however, are so very similar to the hog deer *Axis porcinus* that I personally believe that this deer should be considered as a subspecies of the hog deer. (For the same reason, the Bawean deer might also be considered a subspecies of the hog deer.)

Fortunately, seven Calamian deer (four males and three females) have been caught in Culion and at the time of writing are on their way to England where they will eventually be established in the Port Lympne wildlife sanctuary in Kent—so someone should have the opportunity in due course to decide their true taxonomic status.

So far as Europe is concerned, the only deer whose survival is threatened is the Corsican red deer (*Cervus elaphus corsicanus*), and whilst it

Probably less than a hundred of the southern race of the swamp deer remain in Kanha National Park. Their decline appears to have been caused by poaching and the intrusion of domestic animals into their habitat

The northern race of the swamp deer (above) is much more numerous than the southern, totalling about 4500 animals. This photo was taken in Assam, and the deer also occurs in Uttar Pradesh and western Bengal

The Formosan sika (left) is one of thirteen races of this widely distributed deer. Many of the races are threatened and this particular one may in fact be extinct in the wild

may already be extinct in Corsica, a few still occur in Sardinia, where the total population is probably under 200 animals. On the latter island the deer are protected by regional law, but this has not been adequately enforced and poaching has been the principal cause of their decline.

Farther south, in North Africa, the status of the Barbary deer (*Cervus elaphus barbarus*), which occurs in both Algeria and Tunisia, is rather more encouraging, and indeed a slight increase in numbers has recently occurred in Tunisia where in 1972 the population was estimated to be about 250. There were another 150 in Algeria. Although poaching in the past has been the main cause of decline, the complete protection now afforded is obviously producing results, particularly in Tunisia.

Of the four deer once considered to be at risk in North America, only two—the Columbia white-tailed deer (*Odocoileus virginianus leucurus*) and the Cerros Island mule deer (*Odocoileus hemionus cerrosensis*)—are now endangered. Although there are over twenty other subspecies of white-tail in North America alone, and ten other subspecies of mule deer, both these deer are isolated from other races—the former by geography and the latter by sea. It is not known how many mule deer there are on Cerros Island but it would appear to be not many, for during an official survey carried out in 1972 by the Mexican Wildlife Service, only fresh tracks were seen but no animals. In 1972 the estimated population of Columbia white-tailed deer was put at around 400.

The other two deer once at risk in North America—the tule or dwarf elk (*Cervus canadensis nannodes*) and the Florida Keys white-tailed deer (*Odocoileus virginianus clavium*)—are now considered to be out of danger, and increasing in numbers. The tule elk has always been confined to California, having a great preference for desert conditions, and is now restricted to Owens Valley and a fenced preserve at Tupman, near Bakersfield. The overall population stands at around 500, and indeed some controlled hunting under the jurisdiction of the California Fish and Game Department is now permitted whenever the Owens Valley herds exceed 300, which is considered the maximum the area can hold.

A quarter of a century ago less than forty white-tailed deer were thought to survive in the Florida Keys, their rapid decline having been caused by a combination of excessive hunting, loss of habitat due to human occupation, and casualties caused by hurricanes and flooding. Now the population is estimated to be about 600, which is considered about sufficient for the carrying capacity of the area in the southern Keys where they live.

Four native deer of South America are at present causing some concern, but only one—the pampas deer (*Ozotoceros bezoarticus*), of which there are three subspecies—is considered to be in any real danger. This particularly applies to the Argentine pampas deer, which is now only known to occur in three localities in the wild, where the total population was estimated in 1976 to be under 150 animals. In order to save this deer from extinction a joint conservation project between the provincial authorities of Buenos Aires and the Conseil International de la Chasse was launched in 1976, with the aim of determining 'the feasibility and techniques of re-introducing captive-bred specimens into suitable habitats in the wild' and 'to establish reserves and sanctuaries for the deer'. A captive herd of about twenty-five animals already exists on a private ranch (La Corona) south of Buenos Aires.

Little is known about the status of the other two races of pampas deer—*O. b. bezoarticus* and *O. b. leucogaster*—the former occurring in Brazil and the latter mainly in northern Argentina and adjacent Paraguay, but neither is thought to be faced with near extinction.

The marsh deer (*Blastocerus dichotomus*) is probably not in immediate danger of extinction either. Although its range is much reduced from former times, it is still reported as being 'fairly common' in parts of Bolivia and scattered herds are still present in Peru, Paraguay, Argentina, and Brazil where, in 1971, a population of around 2000 animals was estimated. It is, however, probably extinct in Uruguay.

A deer which is found only in South America is the huemul or guamal of the Andes, of which two species are recognized, *Hippocamelus bisulcus* in the southern Andes of Chile and Argentina, and *H. antisensis* of Ecuador, Peru, Bolivia, and the extreme north-west of Argentina. Although neither is presently endangered there is no doubt that over-hunting has considerably depleted numbers, and though no estimate is available for the northern huemul— known locally as *taruca*—it is doubtful if more than about 1600 south Andean huemuls remain.

Although both deer are legally protected against hunting in much of their range, enforcement is next to impossible in the remote areas in which the two species are found.

And finally, to complete the list of endangered deer, there is the Persian fallow deer—*Dama dama mesopotamica*—a native of Iran and amongst the rarest deer in the world today. Indeed, about forty years ago this deer was declared extinct but fortunately its obituary was a little premature for in 1957 a German by the name of Werner Trense, during a hunting trip in the Khuzistan province of south-west Iran, heard of a deer which answered very closely to the description of a fallow deer. It transpired that this deer was, in fact, the Persian fallow deer and two small herds, each numbering about a dozen animals, were located in the region of the rivers Dez and Karkeh. Following the discovery of this deer a number were subsequently collected, some of which were transferred to a small fenced-in reserve at Dasht-e-Naz near Sari in northern Iran, while a pair were sent to Georg von Opel's private zoo at Kronberg near Frankfurt-am-Main in Germany. Unfortunately the buck died without leaving any progeny, so in order to build up a small herd at Kronberg, the Persian doe was allowed to mate with a common fallow buck.

In 1965 a further pure Persian fallow buck was obtained from Iran, by which time there was at Kronberg, in addition to the pure-bred doe, one buck and three does, all hybrids. Five years later I was informed by letter that there were fourteen 'pure' Persian fallow deer at Kronberg, which seemed a remarkably high number to have achieved from a single pair, unless the pure Persian buck had been allowed to mate with some of the cross-bred does which were at Kronberg when it arrived. What became of these crossbred animals is not known, and although I was assured that none had been sold, I do know for certain that a cross-bred buck—stated to be 75 per cent pure Persian—did reach Munich Zoo from where it was later transferred to Prinz Reuss's wildlife park at Mautern in Austria. This buck was doubtless the cross-bred animal which was at Kronberg at the time (1965) the new buck from Iran had arrived, and was then disposed of. Unfortunately Georg von Opel had died in August 1971 prior to my correspondence with the zoo so it is possible that one or two cross-bred deer

had been disposed of privately and no record kept.

Shortly after Georg von Opel's death, a number of fallow deer from Kronberg were returned to Iran but in a subsequent discussion I had in Tehran with Prince Abdorreza and others, deep concern was being expressed as to whether the animals received from Kronberg could be accepted as being 100 per cent pure-bred Persian fallow deer, particularly as some of the cast antlers suggested otherwise. The antler format of the Persian fallow is a distinctive feature. I was shown a number of cast antlers and when asked for an opinion my only possible reply was that if in doubt they should kill the lot rather than contaminate the existing herd in Iran which was known to be completely pure. To date I do not know what has happened to the deer received from Kronberg but it is to be hoped that any doubtful deer will have been killed.

I have dealt at considerable length with this particular deer for two reasons. In the first place because this animal had already been pronounced extinct, and its 'resurrection from the dead' does give some slight hope that perhaps some other deer—such as Schomburgk's deer from Thailand, which appears to have become extinct at about the same period as the disappearance of the Persian fallow—may have survived in some isolated pocket of country and may one day be rediscovered. Secondly—which is most important—I think the cross-breeding at Kronberg highlights the folly and danger of crossing different species or races in order to build up a herd, and completely nullifies the whole object of trying to create a breeding herd of any rare animal and keep the strain pure. Such crossing, even with a near relative, should only be a very *last* resort and should not be attempted when pure stocks still exist elsewhere, as was the case with the Persian fallow.

The value of collecting some of the world's endangered deer, and placing them in reserves outside their country of origin so that captive-bred specimens can, at some future date, be released in the wild, cannot be over-stressed. As an example, had the 11th Duke of Bedford not had the foresight, some seventy years ago, to collect from the zoos in Europe as many Père David deer as possible for his park at Woburn, this unique Chinese deer would, without question, have been quite extinct today. At

The huemul is much depleted by hunting in the southern Andes, and probably numbers no more than about 1600. No estimate is available for the northern huemul, but it too is probably depleted

Though poaching does take place, the Kashmir stag (top) is slowly increasing in number thanks to strong conservation measures

Thamin or Eld's deer (near right), also known as the brow-antlered deer, is under pressure. Numbers in the Manipur Valley are probably in the hundreds, while the animal's status in Burma is unknown

The number of Florida Keys white-tailed deer (far right) has climbed from about forty to 600 in a quarter century, and the animal is now considered out of danger

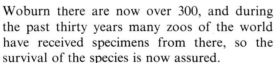

Woburn there are now over 300, and during the past thirty years many zoos of the world have received specimens from there, so the survival of the species is now assured.

The demand for deer antlers for use as an aphrodisiac still exists in the Far East and in the past this has undoubtedly been responsible for the decline in many of the larger Asiatic species of deer, and in particular the Chinese sika. In recent years, however, the creation of deer farms has eased the pressure on the wild herds and some recovery can be expected. The diminutive musk deer, which is a native of the high mountainous forests of Asia, is another deer which may well find salvation in deer farming, for although it carries no antlers it has always been much persecuted for the musk which the male secretes in a sac beneath the skin of its abdomen. Previously it was only possible to collect the musk from a killed specimen but since 1958, when the first experimental musk deer farm was set up, it has been found possible to collect the musk from a living animal. Farming musk deer has, therefore, now become a regular practise, to the obvious benefit of the wild deer.

AFRICA'S DESERT ANTELOPES

by David Black

Unless immediate conservation measures are taken, both the addax antelope and the scimitar-horned oryx will soon be extinct. This was the bleak conclusion of a survey carried out in 1976 by the International Union for Conservation of Nature—and furthermore it is hard to see how large-scale protective measures can be effected considering the vast areas of land involved, with the populations of the two animals scattered over several different countries. Their ranges spread over the Sahara desert and down to the Sahelian zone in the south, a broad belt of arid savanna covering 2600 miles between Mauritania and the Sudan.

The addax is a true desert antelope, at home in the driest areas of the Sahara, especially areas of sand dunes. The oryx, on the other hand, belongs to the Sahelian zone. Both animals are well adapted in their behavior and physiology to life in an arid environment and thus the need to conserve water. Experiments on these and related animals have shown that they can tolerate very high body temperatures, up to 45°C. This means that water, normally lost by sweating in other animals, is conserved. Daily variations of over 10°C have been noted. Efficient oxygen extraction by the lungs and the production of highly concentrated urine also play their part in minimizing water loss.

During the heat of the day, both addax and oryx rest in whatever shade is available. The addax is said to dig out a shallow depression in the sand with its fore-feet. Both species feed and obtain their water requirements at night and during the early morning hours. This period coincides with the time that many desert plants replenish their own water supplies. The plants, like the animals, lose much water during the heat of the day and need to 'top up'

The beautiful scimitar-horned oryx is seriously threatened with extinction. Less than a hundred years ago it was abundant in Morocco, but does not exist there today, or anywhere else north of the Sahara

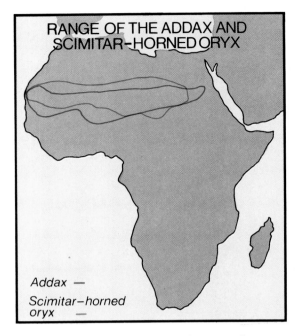

RANGE OF THE ADDAX AND SCIMITAR-HORNED ORYX

Addax —
Scimitar-horned oryx —

their supplies from the underground water table at night. This aspect of water conservation is an example of just one link in the complex relationships of animals and plants in arid zone ecology.

The addax and the oryx were once very common across the Sahara. In ancient Egypt they were domesticated. Stabled like goats, they were bridled, fed from troughs, and probably slaughtered during religious rites. Less than a hundred years ago the scimitar-horned oryx was abundant in Morocco, south of the Atlas Mountains. It does not exist there today, or indeed in any part of its former range north of the great desert.

Both animals represent an important source of protein for the desert tribes, and have always been hunted for their food and skins. The main 'predators' of the oryx are the Haddad tribe of northern Chad, whose entire life and culture depends on this animal. The Haddad have perfected a hunting technique involving men and camels, and they drive the animals into nets made from the leg tendons of the oryx. The animals' reaction when netted is to fight with their horns, with the result that they become even more entangled. The Haddad eat the meat raw, cooked or dried, and the tribe does considerable trade in the dried meat which is often ground into meal. The oryx hide is also very valuable, particularly the skin from the neck region. Other nomadic tribes have evolved systems of running down the oryx on horse-

back and spearing their quarry. These rather primitive hunting methods have given way to more sophisticated slaughter, however, and both addax and oryx have been victims of massive hunting expeditions mounted by local military and the staff of oil companies, who, bored for lack of entertainment, gun down these elegant desert antelopes.

The present status of these two species is roughly as follows. In Mauritania, the situation is critical: the oryx has almost disappeared in the last fifteen years, whereas the addax, protected by the very inhospitable nature of its habitat, is still found in fair numbers, especially near the Mauritania-Mali border, but in greatly reduced numbers since the 5000 estimated in 1960. In neighboring Niger, surveys report a decline in the formerly abundant oryx population. The majority are found between Tadress-Termit and southern Tenere, though some may still survive in the remote valley of Azaouk. The addax again seems to be faring better, and has been reported from the Bilma and Tenere areas of the Sahara from where they periodically migrate north into Algeria.

In the republic of Chad both species are still locally common, with the addax population at around 2500 and the oryx at 5000. Chad is the only country where viable populations of both animals are found, and these are in the vast wildlife reserve of Ouadi-Rimé-Ouadi Achim, situated in the north of the country. This reserve covering some 12 million acres (the size of Scotland) was established in 1969 to protect not only endangered antelopes but other species like the ostrich and the cheetah, this area being at the edge of their range in Africa. The reserve does not have the status of a national park, however, for its management policy is one of compromise between the needs of wildlife and the interests of the local peoples. Arab and Gorene herders of camels, goats, and cattle have unrestricted passage through the reserve. This means that poaching on a large scale occurs, and even more serious is the reduction of pasture land, particularly for the oryx which competes for grazing with the cattle and goats.

Management of the area has been hampered by poor roads and communication difficulties between guards and local tribesmen. Two guard stations were originally set up at towns on the edge of the reserve, but these were too far away from the antelope's main feeding grounds

The Haddad tribe of northern Chad have been the main predators on the scimitar-horned oryx, and their entire life and culture depends on this animal. They have perfected a hunting technique which involves driving the animals into nets made from the leg tendons of . . . oryx

The addax antelope has fared slightly better than the oryx, but it too has declined seriously. Instead of being hunted by traditional methods alone, the new threat is from the modern weapons and transport now found in the most remote parts of the world

for patrolling to be carried out efficiently. Now stations have been located in more suitable sites on the western side of the reserve at the center of the oryx's annual migration route and well within the southern limit of the addax's range. The government has recently increased its assistance in protecting the area by recruiting a further thirty guards, making a total of eighty. Controlled tourism, and the revenue which would result, is the ultimate development which could safeguard the area. The whole reserve is notable for its spectacular variety of desert species as well as the migrant birds which visit in tens of thousands every winter.

East of Chad, in the Sudan, an aerial survey has revealed a few of the smaller desert antelopes like the dorcas and dama gazelles, but there have been no reliable reports of scimitar-horned oryx since 1973, or of addax since 1968.

Hunting with motor vehicles and modern weapons has definitely accelerated the decline of both the addax and the oryx. The antelopes have also retreated because of increased competition from nomadic peoples and their domestic animals. The Sahelian zone has suffered an appalling seven-year drought, which has brought indescribable suffering to the local people. As the scanty grassland pastures have turned to dust, bore holes to tap the underground water have been sunk deep into the interior of the desert. This temporary relief is only followed by further devastation (by invading cattle and goats) of whatever vegetation exists.

A long-term plan to halt the expanding Sahara is urgently called for, and many eminent ecologists advocate the use of native plants and animals (including the addax and oryx) to fit into a plan for increasing the productivity of this arid zone. Efforts by international aid organizations have so far concentrated on trying to restock the area with drought-resistant crops and hardy domesticated animals.

Dr Michael Crawford, of the Nuffield Foundation in London, England, has been one of the pioneers examining the feasibility of managing wild African animals as part of the rehabilitation program and has spent several years in Uganda working on such a scheme. He has repeatedly argued against the use of cattle and other temperate zone animals in such a harsh environment. The productivity of

the arid Sahelian zone in terms of protein from the meat of endemic animals has great potential. All that is needed now is money and persuasion to apply this policy as a pilot scheme in a country like Chad. It is hard to improve upon the intimate balance between desert animals and their food plants.

Both the addax and the scimitar-horned oryx have been bred in captivity. One can see both animals in their natural surroundings at the Hai-Bar reserve in the Negev Desert of Israel. This reserve covers an area of over 8000 acres and is the first of three large nature reserves planned for the country. A breeding nucleus of four scimitar-horned oryx was imported from Denmark in 1970; there are now sixteen animals and the breeding success has been high. Addax imported from the United States have also bred well. Other large animals of the Hai-Bar include the wild ass, gazelle, ostrich, hyena, and desert lynx.

In Europe an important breeding center for the scimitar-horned oryx is Marwell Zoological Park in Hampshire, England, managed by John Knowles, who has an excellent record in breeding endangered animals. Here the oryx takes pride of place; its breeding behavior has been well documented, and great care has been taken in the rearing of the young. The horn buds of the calves are soft during the first few weeks of life and are very susceptible to damage, but careful husbandry has prevented any deformities. There is a herd of twenty-five animals at Marwell now and they share a large paddock area with Grevy's zebras, ostriches, and crowned cranes.

The status of the addax and the scimitar-horned oryx highlights the critical situation of the trans-Sahelian zone. There are many other desert and arid grassland species that are in danger as the whole habitat becomes in turn eroded and then invaded by the hungry local tribes who, like the animals, have to scratch a living from the poor earth. It is only with broadly based conservation measures that the area can live again. It is hoped that the governments concerned, with the help of conservation organizations, will succeed in saving the populations of addax and oryx, at present so seriously threatened with extinction.

ON THE TRACKS OF THE IRIOMOTE CAT

by Yoshinori Imaizumi

Some thirteen years ago, in 1964, a new cat was discovered on remote Iriomotejima Island in the Ryukyu group. The discovery caused great excitement throughout the world not only because it is rare for a higher animal to be discovered nowadays but also because the Iriomote cat appeared to be the most primitive member of the cat family.

Iriomotejima is one of Japan's last unexploited regions. The second-largest island in the Okinawa Prefecture, it measures about nineteen miles from east to west and thirteen miles from north to south. Some hamlets lie scattered along the east and west coasts, but there is no road between east and west, the whole island being mountainous with subtropical rain forest. Attempts have been made to cultivate parts of the island, but the difficult terrain has so far prevented too much settlement. Here, in these virgin forests, lives *Mayailurus iriomotensis*, the Iriomote wild cat.

It is a sad fact, however, that any reasonably large animal that is newly discovered today is likely to be declared in danger of extinction almost in the same breath! The question therefore was: would the Iriomote cat be safe if the future development of the island proceeded in a controlled manner? One argument was that since the animals had survived there for millions of years, they would be able to continue to survive in the future. But this is not valid, for there are today many new factors which endanger the wildlife of Iriomote—domestic cats, pet dogs, increasing road traffic, and the introduction of diseases and parasites which cannot be controlled. Should any of these factors get out of hand the entire species—it is also in a genus of its own—could easily become extinct in a short period. Immediate action was

A new species of wild cat was discovered in 1964 on Iriomotejima Island in the Ryukyu group. The new cat appeared to be the most primitive member of the cat family. But how many of them were there? There could not have been very many because their island home only measures some nineteen by thirteen miles

therefore necessary to protect the cat while there was still time. But before action could be taken more information was needed, and so a research team was sent to the island at the request of the Environment Agency of Japan.

The main objects of the investigation were to find out the number of cats; their range on the island; their feeding and breeding habits; and the environmental requirements for their survival. Their range and requirements could be established through the distribution of footprints and feces; feeding habits by analysis of the feces; and the quantity of food required by various research efforts involving both wild and captive cats.

The droppings of Iriomote cats are usually found on bare ground or on boulders along the roads, and they are not covered with earth like the feces of domestic cats. The animals are thus fairly easily tracked. Moreover, thanks to the feline habit of cleaning by licking, there is almost always a trace of hair in the droppings which makes it easier (from the differences in the hair) to distinguish the wild cats from their domestic cousins.

Breeding behavior, however, is not easy to investigate and so far we have had no success in this direction. A more urgent task is to make an accurate estimate of the numbers of the cat population, and ascertain the scope of its activities. And this is not merely urgent but very difficult.

Telemetry—by which 'bugged' animals are tracked by aircraft—has been used with great success with a number of mammals elsewhere, and this technique would certainly be ideal for our research. In practise, however, there are problems. First of all we would have to catch some cats (three, to be sure of the results) and attach radio transmitters to them. Catching the wild cats alive would be very difficult, if not impossible. And if we did manage to catch any, could we pick up their transmissions successfully? For reasons I shall discuss, this seems very doubtful.

The island of Iriomote has a large number of rivers, some of which are surprisingly big considering the size of the island (about 112 square miles). There are more than thirty rivers, among them the Nakama which is about 100 miles long and flows down to the east coast. The island is composed largely of sandstone, sandy dirt-bed, and conglomerate, and is therefore easily furrowed by these rivers which slice deep and divide the gentle, hilly terrain into many plateaux. Nakama Peninsula, on the northern bank of the Nakama River, looks deceptively like a flat plain dotted by clumps of young Ryukyu pines. Many buffalo-cart tracks, which branch off from the main east-coast road, are flanked by rows of trees six to nine feet high. These innocent-looking trees are, in fact, extremely treacherous for behind them are hidden narrow ravines 120 feet deep and covered with dark, dense jungle. There are about six ravines like this in the area we chose for our investigation. These forest-covered ravines provide excellent cover for the wild cats, which are thoroughly at home there.

It was obvious that transmitter signals would not reach us unless we could use elaborate methods, perhaps with the help of an aircraft. But we had neither the time nor the money to spend on aircraft.

So what was to be done? Could we use dogs, such as beagles, to follow the wild cats' tracks? There are many paths, tunnelled through tightly knitted, thorny thickets by small Ryukyu wild boar; the wild cats can make use of them, but not beagles, which are too big for the narrow, thorny tunnels. There are also poisonous snakes lurking in the thickets. Even if the beagles overcame these physical obstacles, they might not be able to follow the track of a single cat: they might switch from the scent of one cat to that of another, and our results would be meaningless.

Throughout the preliminary investigations of 1973 and 1974 I was made to realize again and again how difficult it is to observe the wild cat. When we had chosen a feeding-spot, we would put up a blind nearby in order to make observations as soon as the cat had got used to the situation. We would soon know that a cat was visiting the spot regularly every night because the food would start disappearing. Then one night we would creep in behind the blind. No cat. It is known that feline species have better hearing than, say, canines. But I have now come to believe that the Iriomote cat must be able to hear the human heart-beat!

But though the cats are extremely suspicious of human beings, they do not pay much attention to mechanical objects. Cameras, strobe lights, and clocks were virtually ignored after a cursory inspection. We considered this a splendid bonus and decided to take automatic photographs to identify individual cats.

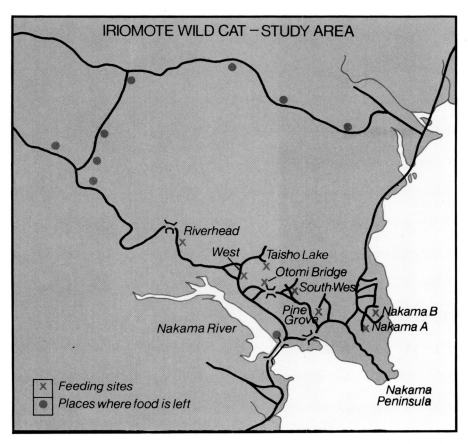

IRIOMOTE WILD CAT – STUDY AREA

Riverhead

West Taisho Lake
Otomi Bridge
South-West

Pine Grove
Nakama B
Nakama A

Nakama River

Nakama Peninsula

✗ Feeding sites
● Places where food is left

When feeding, the cats do not chew but instead swallow a big piece of meat in one gulp. This proved to be a useful habit for us, because we could put some identifying matter in the feed and try to trace it later on. By combining photo-identification with marked food, we felt we should be able to find out something about their activities. But what could be used to mark the food? On the one hand it had to be indigestible, yet, more important, it had to be harmless. At home I had been experimenting with a small bit of Dymotape (embossed plastic labelling tape), buried in a chunk of meat, which I fed to a stray cat. It was delighted, particularly when I continued the experiment for two weeks, and it thrived on the diet. When we used the same technique on a captive Iriomote wild cat it readily ate the food. We examined the marker passed through in the feces and found it to be in perfect condition without discoloration; even the letter embossed on it was clearly legible. This, we agreed, must be the method for our field work.

During the preliminary feeding experiments we set up four feeding spots along the east coast road and had success at three of them. So when we started the investigation itself we decided to use the same area. In November 1974, however, we found to our dismay that the northernmost part of the feeding area had been enclosed inside barbed-wire fencing for a cattle grazing field. When two more feeding sites to the south had become unavailable for various reasons, we re-examined the area and decided that after all it was not suitable.

In the first place, all the sites were located on a strip of land about half a mile inland from the coast and the terrain beyond this line would be difficult to penetrate. In winter one of the cats which visited a feeding site here used to come down the hill and cross the main road to hunt for wild duck by a small lake near the beach; then in the morning it would return to the hill along a buffalo-cart track. Soon after we had started our preliminary observations at this spot, a group of workmen arrived. They began erecting the barbed-wire fencing for the cattle only four yards from the observation point, so for the remainder of the observation period Professor Paul Leyhausen (of Germany) had to keep watch sitting inside the barbed wire. A man in a cage looking for a wild animal!

The workmen arrived about 8.30 in the morning on their bicycles and left at 5.00 in the evening. During the observation period the cat did not alter its routine of a daily descent from the hilly hide-out. On one occasion it went right down to the lake by the beach. One morning, after a heavy night's rainfall, we were on our way to the observation site when we saw the cat's footmarks clearly imprinted on the fresh tire-tracks of the workmen's bicycles. We followed them for 700 yards towards the dense jungle of the hill. Professor Leyhausen estimated then that a cat's territory must be about 250 acres.

We were still thinking of adopting this site for our investigation. But by early summer, we found that the feeding site was not being used so often and after a while there were no signs of the cat at all, either at the site or by the lake below. Clearly the cat's behavior changed from season to season, and so we needed to include mountain areas in our observation to understand the animal's movements throughout the year.

It took us a long time to decide on the best observation area, but finally we chose an area of about 1780 acres, including Nakama Peninsula. Here we set up eight separate feeding sites. We began to attract the cats to the sites by using live chickens as bait. It took them an average of 8.3 days to get to the chickens (of course, all eight started their feeding at different times).

On 11 December 1974 the first cat started to feed on marked meat at the south-west site. It swallowed about twenty pieces of Dymo altogether on the 11th, 15th, 18th, 20th, 22nd, and successive days. But we were quite unable to find the markers! What had gone wrong? Would it prove impossible to recover them?

Our days were packed with things to be done. We had been given a jeep by the World Wildlife Fund, but even with the help of this vehicle it was a physical ordeal to cover ninety miles a day, checking and replacing the feed where necessary and resetting the cameras. And how it rains on Iriomote island! In December, on average, there are twenty days of rain, and in between the rainstorms come showers with strong winds. We had to rig up shelters to protect the cameras from rain and wind: an umbrella was attached to the tripod and the camera was wrapped in plastic sheeting beneath it. Every morning we had to collect the photographic equipment to avoid it being damaged by wild visitors and then set up the cameras again in the evening.

In between these routine chores, we had to grope around looking for droppings. Another pressing task at this stage was to complete an accurate map of the area since the existing map was far from correct. And then another search for droppings. We did not allow ourselves to look up as we walked about, and even to go about bent double with eyes wide open was not sufficient: we had to learn to smell the cat's scent as well. In addition to its footprints we were seeking the animal's 'signposts'.

The Iriomote cat's urine has an extremely strong smell, and like busy hounds we would sniff along after the scent. Then suddenly the most powerful odor would hit us. The site for the signpost might be a stone or the broken trunk of a tree or just a clump of grass—nor were our tripods, the strobe battery cases, or even rat-traps exempt from the cat's obsessive signposting. Unfortunately, there is a tree called *soshiju*, a member of the acacia family with thin willow-like leaves, which has a smell very similar to that of the cat's urine. We called this 'the cat tree'. How many times did we follow the cat's trail with zeal, only to find ourselves

The Iriomote cats were photographed many times feeding on bait. Pieces of colored plastic tape were embedded in the bait so that when they were excreted the scientists would be able to get an idea of the animals' travels. The cats themselves triggered the cameras automatically

standing in front of a cat tree.

This was by no means all of our work in the field. Often we would encounter other creatures as we made our daily rounds. To get to know the cat's natural environment, we felt we must make the acquaintance of its fellow inhabitants. So we would squat over a marshy pool in dark jungle, being bitten by gnats and waiting patiently for a frog to appear. There are just too many rare animals and birds on Iriomote, and too often our daily routine was disturbed while we took photographs of a rare bird or an unusual insect.

So the days passed, but never a Dymo marker did we discover. I was due to return to Japan on the 25th and I began to worry. I desperately wanted to be sure that the feeding method was working. If it proved successful, then we proposed to carry on with it for a year. If not, we had to think of an alternative. As a matter of fact, we were experimenting with another method during this period. We had discovered that the cat had a habit of carrying off the feed to eat it in a safer place—sometimes as far as fifty yards away—and we thought that we might make use of this habit to discover its den. When we used chicken as bait, we found a trail of white feathers on the ground which we were able to follow to a cave on top of a 200-foot-deep ravine. So we attached the next feed to a reel of strong plastic string and fastened the reel to a tree, hoping that the cat would carry off the feed in its mouth and pull out the string behind it, thus leaving us an easy trail to follow. But the experiment failed. Although in earlier tests the combined strength of two men in a tug of war had failed to break the string, the cat's sharp teeth had cut right through it! We went back to our camp much discouraged, only to find that the long-awaited good news had arrived.

On 24 December on a strip of bare land two ravines away from the south-west feeding site some bright orange-colored markers were found. They had been in food taken by a cat on the 20th and were discovered 120 yards away from the feeding site in a direct line. It was not difficult to find out how the cat had actually travelled to the spot. We worked backwards from the droppings to the feeding site along the route we presumed the cat had taken. At the end of the bare land we turned east to find a sheer cliff going down, thickly covered with forest. At the bottom of the cliff was a stream about two yards wide, which was soon joined by another stream to become much wider and occupy the whole width of the bottom of the ravine. Unable to go any farther, we climbed up on the other side to find a well-trodden path through a thick wall of bushes.

After this came a jungle of Pandanus with blade-sharp leaves and roots spread far and wide. Then came a steep climb through masses of tall *tokiwa* pampas grass. By the time we reached the feeding site our hands were scratched and bleeding. But we were well pleased: the feeding method had proved successful and good enough to continue for the next year.

Two younger members of our team were assigned to continue the routine checking and collection of markers. The marker collection continued smoothly with five retrieved in December, eight in January, thirty-nine in February . . . The photo-identification process went smoothly too, and by March 1975 we had no fewer than 180 photographs of wild cats which regularly visited our feeding sites.

Professor Leyhausen estimated when we began our research that the total number of Iriomote cats would be about 300. But when he saw the island and realized that villages and agricultural land occupied more space than he had envisaged, he lowered his estimate to 150. The Japanese team estimated a total cat population of between 135 and 154 in the spring of 1975. These figures, based on our preliminary observations, suggested an area of 500 to 680 acres of land per wild cat, and agreed with Professor Leyhausen's estimate. But even at that time we expressed pessimism about our own estimate, because our preliminary feeding sites were located in the plateaux and not in the mountains, where the natural density of distribution would be less.

The data gathered during the summer months confirmed our fears. Generally the wild cats only come down to the plateaux in winter; in the spring they disappear into their individual mountain territories where they spend the summer and autumn months. This habit calls for further investigation and clearly we must find out more about their summer territorial distribution.

Research is still in progress as I write, and we cannot yet come to any definite conclusion. But from the evidence we have accumulated so far we should say that the distribution of the Iriomote wild cat is as low as one to every 1730 acres. There are only some 68,700 acres (107 square miles) of habitat on the island suitable for the wild cats. This means that only forty—perhaps fewer—cats are still in existence. We can say for certain that the Iriomote wild cat is in greater danger than we had imagined.

BATS AT RISK

by Robert Stebbing

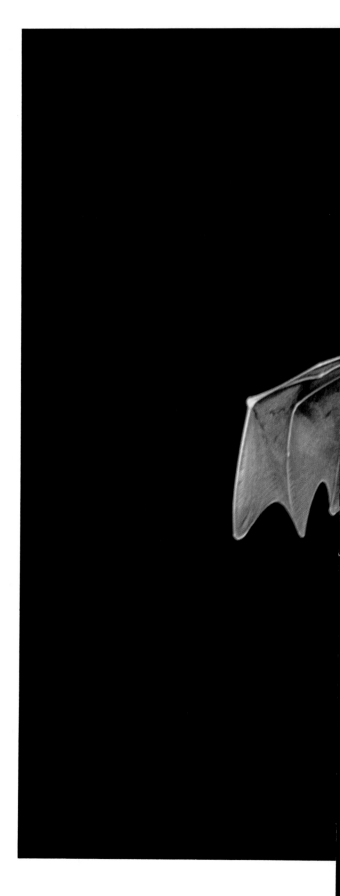

There are about 850 species of bats in the world and about one tenth of these occur in cooler temperate regions. In Britain, the fifteen resident species represent nearly one third of the country's indigenous mammals.

While some bats feed on fruit (some specializing on nectar and pollen), meat and fish, and everyone has heard of the notorious blood drinking vampires, most species feed on insects. In temperate areas all are insectivorous. Because of the highly seasonal nature of insect abundance, the behavior and physiology of bats have become adapted to coping with lack of food. Some, like the Mexican freetail bats, spend the summer in the south-western United States, but migrate south in the fall so as to be able to continue feeding. A few of these freetails stay in Texas and hibernate. Most temperate species hibernate rather than migrate. However, some bats, particularly in eastern Europe, migrate up to 1250 miles to warmer areas, but this is in order to find suitable hibernation sites which will remain above freezing. In Britain, western Europe, and North America most species move only a few miles rather than hundreds from summer to winter roosts.

Temperate bats cannot be considered as ordinary mammals because of their specialized physiology. Unlike most mammals, bats do not regulate their bodies to a steady temperature but normally approximate their surroundings. This is advantageous to them because during periods of low food availability they avoid activity and thus conserve their reserves of fat. Bats actively and very critically select their roosting environment (their requirements including a particular location, shape, size, temperature, and humidity). The choice varies seasonally and depends on many factors in-

The greater horseshoe bat now has legal protection in Britain. It has undergone very substantial reductions in range, and its population has declined from many thousands a century ago to barely one thousand today

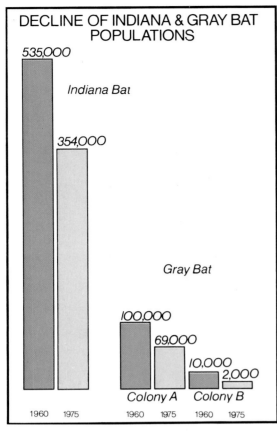

DECLINE OF INDIANA & GRAY BAT POPULATIONS

535,000
Indiana Bat

354,000

Gray Bat

100,000
69,000
10,000
2,000

Colony A   Colony B

1960   1975   1960   1975   1960   1975

cluding the bats' age, sex, weight, and past experience.

At the beginning of hibernation higher temperatures are preferred than at the end and generally (but not invariably) old adult females prefer the highest and juvenile males the lowest temperatures. High humidities are essential to prevent dessication of their wing membranes.

In Europe the greater horseshoe bat prefers the highest hibernation temperatures of up to 12 °C and tends to be gregarious, while at the other extreme, barbastelles roost solitarily in cold sites around 0 °C. In North America the red bat withstands body temperatures as low as –5 °C.

In the fall bats rapidly accumulate fat, which can amount to thirty per cent of their body weight, and this is metabolized during hibernation. Bats wake periodically throughout hibernation, take short flights, and often select different positions in which to continue hibernating. If suitable sites within one roost are not available then they fly to other areas.

Some sites (especially for highly colonial species) can be very important for whole regional populations. In Vermont, for example,

one cave contains about 300,000 little brown bats. These gather from at least 8500 square miles. Therefore, if the entrance was blocked during the winter this species would virtually cease to exist in New England. While in Britain no very large hibernation colonies are known it is still evident that regional populations gather from a few hundred square miles into single clusters.

In spring, bats usually move into various transition roosts before adult females segregate into nursery roosts. These roosts can also contain regional populations and this makes them very vulnerable to various catastrophes. Pregnant female greater horseshoe bats in Dorset, in southern England, gather in one roost from an area of about 700 square miles. Nursery roosts characteristically have high temperatures due either to their location in a building or because of the large number of clustered bats. Although temperatures between 30 °C and 35 °C are usually preferred, under black slates or corrugated iron temperatures may reach 60 °C. Some body temperatures can exceed 50 °C for short periods but generally they are kept below 42 °C.

Mating occurs mostly in September but continues throughout the winter. Females store the sperm, and ovulation and fertilization takes place in April or May. Gestation averages fifty days but can be up to ninety days. Normally only one young is born annually to each adult female but a few species produce twins. The genus Lasiurus in North America is unusual in generally producing three, and sometimes four, young. Weaning takes twenty-five to fifty days and juveniles reach adult size in sixty days. Maximum weight is attained by the end of their third year.

Females of most species reach maturity in their second year, but some breed in their first year and others in their third, and greater horseshoes often in their fourth. Bats are long lived, with many reaching fifteen years and exceptionally up to twenty-four years.

Thus bats have adapted to living in temperate climates by evolving a highly specialized metabolism which allows them to shut-down when food is scarce. But man has influenced some species, causing their decline.

Parallel with the ever-changing climate have been changes in distribution of flora and fauna. Since the last Ice Age large changes must have occurred in the relative abundance and dis-

Two bat conservation projects in Britain: the grille across the mouth of a Devon cave allows bats free passage but keeps out humans, while the bat box is part of a World Wildlife Fund project to find out if man-made roosting sites would be beneficial

(Overleaf) Greater horseshoe bats in hibernation. When hibernating, the immature bats form large clusters, while the adults hang in smaller groups or alone

tribution of all bat species. Such changes will still be taking place. However, now that man in densely populated regions such as Europe and North America has such a controlling influence over the pattern of habitat change, it is difficult to isolate those induced by man from those occurring due to natural causes. Also, some bats appear to be adapting to new roosts, while others are not.

In Britain, during the past 3000 years, large areas of forest have been felled, fragmented, and replaced by agricultural and grazing lands. With the increase in human population came new roosts and habitat in the form of urban development, while tree holes became scarcer. With the Industrial Revolution vast lengths of mine tunnels were dug, often in areas devoid of natural caves. The overall result of these changes was that species depending on high forest and tree holes probably declined in numbers while cave dwelling bats probably increased. And those bats that moved into buildings and urban habitats probably became more plentiful. The pattern of gradual change probably continued into this century, but we have no precise knowledge of population changes for any species. However, let us look at the two species now protected by law in Britain.

The greater horseshoe bat was present throughout southern England and half of Wales in the nineteenth century. In south-east England sizeable colonies used to breed in several cathedrals and tunnels. The species is now absent from that region.

It seems probable that breeding colonies were at one time confined to the natural limestone caves of Wales and western England but that cathedrals (e.g. Wells Cathedral) were used later. Mine tunnels dug in caveless areas of southern England opened up new territories and were duly colonized, but during the past century and a half bats have been excluded from cathedrals and cave colonies have been disturbed by naturalists, commercialization, and recently by cavers. Now no breeding colonies exist in either caves or cathedrals but are confined to large houses. Greater horseshoes in hibernation form large clusters, mostly of immature bats, while adults hang in small groups or singly. Many individual old adults occupy the same mines each winter and members of one colony may be spread between tens of locations. This makes it difficult to select priorities for site protection. Also, a site may be used only for a few days each year, but be nonetheless vital for a particular stage of the animal's life history.

The greater horseshoe was given legislative protection in 1975 for several reasons. First, it had undergone substantial reductions in range. Second, populations which almost certainly totalled many thousands a century ago now number only a little over one thousand. Thirdly, this species is very conspicuous in caves and is used extensively for experimental work. It has also been collected. In mainland Europe the greater horseshoe has virtually disappeared from Holland, Belgium, northern France, and central Germany, but it is still reasonably common in southern Europe.

The second totally protected species in Britain is the mouse-eared bat. However, this animal is in a different category because it is a recent colonist of Britain. It first arrived in the 1950s in Dorset where a small colony of about ten bats tried to establish themselves. Then in the late 1960s a larger colony of about twenty-five was discovered in Sussex. Bats in Dorset were frequently disturbed, and some collected, so that no viable colony is known today. In Sussex protective measures were instigated very quickly and it is hoped the colony will increase.

In Europe, mouse-eareds were once common in Belgium, Holland, northern Germany, and northern France, with very large colonies, but now they are either extinct or very rare. Some

large colonies are still found in southern Europe.

The main causes of the decline of both species are destruction of both breeding and hibernation cave roosts by cement industries, killing by fumigation of colonies in buildings, collecting bats for experimental work, and the disturbance of colonies by tourists, cavers, and naturalists.

All other species in Britain may have declined in the past quarter century but we have no accurate figures. Many people have reported seeing fewer noctules, and this could be due to both the reduction in numbers of hollow trees and large insects. In Czechoslovakia, a similar decline has been noted. Lesser horseshoes in Britain and Europe have become much rarer but no measure exists of the size of this decline.

In Europe as a whole no species is threatened with extinction although in individual countries some have died out. This is probably more serious in the long term than it at first appears. The greater horseshoe colonies in Britain were probably continuous with populations in Belgium, Holland, and France, with some interchange. Now fragmentation of populations prevents any possibility of interchange and the smaller colony size is probably reducing survival. Current research is aimed at understanding the detailed environmental requirements of these bats so that in the long term optimum conditions can be provided.

In North America several species are now considered endangered. This designation was given because of the declines that had occurred in some areas even though large populations still existed.

The Indiana bat, which hibernates in very tight clusters in caves, suffered a population decline of thirty-four per cent from 535,000 in 1960 to 354,000 in 1975. Many of the usual causes could be implicated, such as disturbance and loss of roosts, but vandalism and loss of feeding habitat appears to have had important consequences. One cave was visited in 1961 by people carrying flaming torches and 10,000 bats were killed. Instances of rock throwing have accounted for large numbers of bats. Little is known about the summer roosts of this species but it seems to form small colonies in hollow trees and beneath loose bark in river flood plains. Channeling of rivers and changes in managing this habitat have probably already helped to reduce populations, and the controversial Meramec dams will not only destroy much critical habitat but also flood some of the hibernation caves.

A second endangered species, the gray bat, occupies part of the same range as the Indiana bat. Although it shares similar feeding habitats along rivers, it spends the whole year roosting in large clusters in caves. Two colonies declined from 100,000 and 10,000 in 1960 to 69,000 and under 2000 in 1975. Disturbance by people seems to have caused these losses. It has been recommended that one visit each second year is the maximum permissible even for census work.

Another species, the Mexican free-tailed bat, although not yet on the official endangered list has experienced spectacular declines. About 8,700,000 were estimated to live at Carlsbad Cavern, New Mexico, in 1937. But in 1973 only 200,000 were counted. Similarly, Eagle Creek Cave, Arizona, had peak numbers of about 25 million bats in 1964 but by 1970 only 600,000 remained. The total population living in the south-west United States in the 1950s was about 200 million but now only a few million remain. The major cause appeared to be pesticides but other factors, including disease, may have been involved.

Although some declines can be attributed directly to vandalism, collecting, destruction of roosts, or poisoning by pesticides, not all can be explained in that way. It is likely that gross changes in habitats and agricultural practises as well as known reductions in insect abundance will have affected survival and breeding success. If bats have to fly farther to catch each insect then the extra energy involved will not be available to feed young or put on fat for hibernation.

Legislation cannot prevent all changes in land-use, but it can help prevent deliberate disturbance, removal by experimenters, or collecting. It can also be used to help persuade landowners or homeowners that the colonies they shelter require protection. Also legislation covering endangered species has a great educational value in highlighting some of the problems, and, it is hoped, could lead to the next generation being much more sympathetic towards protecting wildlife.

Once it is established that a species has declined, and that certain roosts and habitats are critical for its life history, action can be taken to protect the sites and if necessary im-

Hibernation sites are very important for gregarious bats. The greater horseshoe (above) gathers from an area of about 700 square miles to roost in one cave in southern England. The little brown bat (left) gathers from some 8500 square miles to one Vermont cave which contains about 300,000 of them in winter

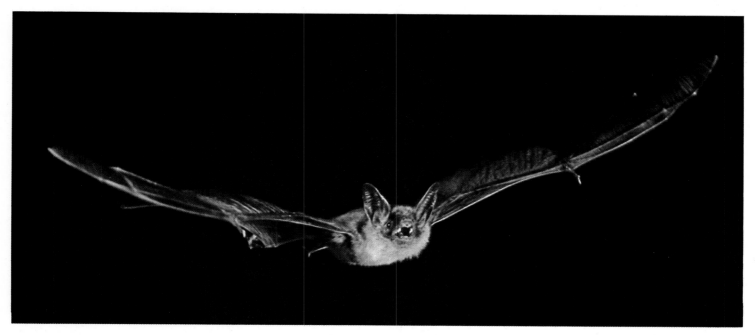

The mouse-eared bat (above) is a recent colonist of Britain, arriving from Europe in the 1950s. It is now totally protected

prove or provide others. Caves and mines are relatively easy to protect in principle but in practise many problems are encountered. Sport caving is a major leisure activity and since the number of available caves is limited, blocking some entrances with grilles would not stop determined cavers from entering. In most instances, however, co-operation of local caving clubs (when it has been sought) has resulted in the club members doing the necessary work and then limiting their caving activity to the summer months when bats are absent. Unfortunately, caves which are used for breeding as well as hibernation must be closed to people at all times. Species like the greater horseshoe bat visit an enormous number of sites each year and because of the large costs involved in grilling, only a few of the most important can be protected.

The greater horseshoe in Britain used to breed in caves (as it still does in southern Europe) but all nurseries are now in buildings. Some of these are derelict and in a state of collapse and the only solution seems to be to provide purpose-built roosts. Unfortunately, not only will this be expensive but it is a gamble whether the right environment can be recreated. It would have been desirable to try this out for a common bat before having to do it for an endangered species. Further research is needed to establish the relative importance of certain types of habitat in the life history of endangered species so that if necessary some feeding areas

can be protected and managed.

In some habitats, such as conifer forest, lack of roost sites may be limiting the number of bats. Experiments are in progress to establish whether providing roost boxes can increase both the number of bats and the range of species. It is possible that some rare species, like Bechstein's bat, may be limited by the lack of suitable roosts in large forests and may benefit by the addition of these boxes.

Following the introduction of protective legislation there has been an increased public awareness of the plight of bats, and much money and help have been provided. Let us hope this impetus can be maintained.

BIRDS

OPERATION OSPREY

by Michael Everett

August 2, 1959, is an important date in the history of bird protection in Britain. It is doubtful whether very many birdwatchers or even conservationists know why—and as far as I am aware there is no annual celebration of it even among those who do. But something significant did happen on that day nearly two decades ago: a young osprey made its first flight from an eyrie on a tall Scots pine on Speyside, in Scotland. Within a day or two, another pair had left the nest, marking a successful end to a venture which was without precedent in the annals of bird protection. The venture was called 'Operation Osprey' and had made history.

To see why Operation Osprey had been necessary in the first place, we must go back in time and take a brief look at the status of the osprey as a British breeding bird. Unfortunately, the literature is so scanty and incomplete, particularly before 1800, that it is virtually impossible to know how common or wide-spread the bird was in centuries past— but from the few clues we have we can deduce that it must have been a reasonably familiar bird in some parts of England, and may have been much more numerous in Scotland. What is certain is that by 1850 it had vanished from its last English haunts (in the West Country)

and was already becoming something of a rarity in Scotland. During the latter half of the last century, collectors of eggs and specimens were putting the finishing touches to a steady process of extirpation begun long before by the sporting fraternity and their gamekeepers. Like all birds of prey in the Victorian period, ospreys were classed as vermin and were persecuted accordingly; and then when specimens and clutches of eggs came to have a rarity value the collectors moved in.

Space does not permit an account of the last stand of the Scottish ospreys, of the efforts of men like the Grants of Rothiemurchus and the Camerons of Locheil to save them, or of the often fantastic exploits of the collectors and their agents. A few pairs managed to survive for some time despite the odds ranged against them. The picturesque site on the Wolf of Badenoch's ruined castle in Loch an Eilein was last used in 1899 (the last Speyside breeding record), while that in an oak on a small island in Loch Arkaig, Argyll, survived until 1908. It is just possible that a pair bred in Sutherland in 1910 (where the last definite record was in 1850) and another Argyll site, at Loch Loyne, was used until 1916. The story ends there, apart from an unsubstantiated rumor of breeding along the Aberdeen-Banff border in 1925 and an unsuccessful attempt at reintroduction (using American birds) made by Captain C. W. R. Knight at Loch Arkaig in 1929.

For many years, ospreys occurred in Scotland only as rare passage migrants, but by the early 1950s it was apparent that rather more birds were passing through (and that these were still being shot and trapped with some regularity). A few optimists even dared to hope that some of these Scandinavian migrants might stay to breed—with good reason, we now know, although many laughed at their ideas at the time.

Secrecy and controversy surrounded the events of 1954 for many years, but it is now

Though relatively abundant in some parts of the world, the osprey vanished from Scotland between 1916 and 1954, thanks largely to the activities of egg collectors who completed a process of extermination begun by sportsmen

accepted that a pair of ospreys bred success-fully on Speyside that year and fledged two young. Following this, single pairs built nests at Loch Garten in 1955 and in Rothiemurchus Forest in 1956, but the evidence points to robbery by egg-collectors in both years. In 1957 a single bird repaired and lined the Loch Garten eyrie, but no mate appeared.

It seemed a fair bet that the ospreys would try again, and sure enough 1958 saw a pair back at the Loch Garten site. This time, a small, determined band of watchers from the Royal Society for the Protection of Birds (RSPB) was there in readiness: by later standards, they were few in number, much over-worked and living in fairly primitive condi-tions, but they were hopeful of success. Their critics of later years (and there have been quite a number of them) would do well to consider that these men were pioneers, assembled at short notice and in many cases helping out in their spare time, with little previous practical experience to fall back on. Manpower and money were in short supply and the scale of their operations was limited by an overriding need for strict secrecy.

The sad events of that first season have been recorded by Philip Brown who was then Secretary of the RSPB. It was his misfortune, and that of Bert Axell, who had hurried north to help, to be on watch overnight when an egg-collector climbed the tree. The two men blundered across the wet bog in the darkness, disturbed the collector, and gave chase: he was not apprehended and even though there was a broken egg below the eyrie it still held two eggs and all seemed well. Imagine the bitter dis-appointment and frustration felt by the small group of wardens next day when they found the nest contained two domestic hens' eggs crudely marked with brown shoe polish . . .

So far, then, five seasons had gone by and, since the details of the successful breeding in 1954 were still vague at that time, it seemed that the ospreys' attempts to re-establish them-selves were doomed to failure unless an even greater effort was made to help them. But by a curious twist of fate, the 1958 disaster had one interesting spin-off. In common with the robbed ospreys of previous seasons, the birds moved elsewhere and built a 'frustration eyrie' in another tree near Loch Garten. It was a Scots pine, and not a particularly handsome one at that, and it was to this tree that the

birds came in 1959 to construct an eyrie which has become the best-known bird's nest in Britain.

By the spring of 1959, the osprey story had become public knowledge and it was clear to the RSPB that additional protective measures were not all that had to be taken into account: there was the problem of more and more bird-watchers wanting to know and see what was going on. The solution here was simply to ask for their help as voluntary wardens—the response was enormous and from now on man-power problems became almost a thing of the past. A camp was set up at Inchdryne Farm, near Loch Garten, with tented accommoda-tion, a caravan for meals, and a sectional hut used as a common room. The pattern for following years was established with a nucleus of paid staff—one or two wardens plus a cook-caterer—aided by relays of volunteers who kept watch on the eyrie and in due course became guides to the public as well.

Meanwhile, the eyrie tree received some attention—its lower branches were removed and the trunk was swathed in great coils of barbed wire. A 'forward hide' or blind was set up for the wardens and a little later a duckboard path was laid from here to the tree; the events of 1958 had shown how necessary it was to be able to get out there quickly should the need arise. In later years, electronic warning devices became very much a feature of this forward position. Last, but by no means least, dis-

A male osprey approaches its nest carrying a fish, and (right) an osprey in a roosting tree in Sweden. Ospreys bred in Scotland until 1916, but after that there was a long gap until 1954 when a pair of Scandinavian passage migrants decided not to pass through

cussions with the owners of the area, the Sea-field Estates, led to the establishment of an RSPB reserve over 667 acres around the eyrie. The Society's position was strengthened considerably when a Sanctuary Order under the 1954 Protection of Birds Act made it an offense to enter the reserve between April and July without RSPB permission.

All went well, culminating in the fledging of the three young in August, by which time some 14,000 people had seen the birds. The decision to open the reserve to visitors was taken after the young had hatched, but not without some misgivings. In the event, the RSPB scored a double success in 1959, showing that with carefully controlled access people could be brought in to see rare breeding birds without disturbing them at all. Indeed, the ospreys soon became used to the comings and

goings of the wardens and visitors, most of whom must be in full view from the eyrie.

Since that first wonderful year, the ospreys have returned annually to the Garten eyrie. Two young were reared there in 1976 to bring the grand total since 1959 up to 32. Operation Osprey has not been trouble-free though: in both 1963 and 1966 gales destroyed the nest and there was no successful breeding; 1975 was also a blank year when an apparently inexperienced female failed to build a complete nest. Before the 1964 season we discovered that vandals had sawn through the trunk of the nest tree. Since then, the old pine has been held up by large iron bars secured by bolts! Operations of this kind, run by experienced people both on site and behind the scenes, soon begin to progress smoothly and almost automatically, so that there can be a real danger of complacency

creeping in. Just how real this danger can be came home to us in 1971 when the ospreys' eggs were taken one night, right under the wardens' noses! This also demonstrated very clearly that even a pair of stringently-protected rare birds can be robbed by determined egg-collectors. The subsequent revision of security measures was probably a good thing: it kept us on our toes and certainly the robbery itself re-awakened public interest in the ospreys.

Public interest and support has undoubtedly been a major factor in the success story of the Loch Garten ospreys. Over the years, facilities for visitors have been improved and expanded so much that wardens from the early days would hardly recognize Operation Osprey as being the same scheme they knew years ago. Close to a million people have now been to this reserve and the value to the conservation movement of the sympathy and understanding that has resulted should not be underestimated. In recent years it has become fashionable in some quarters to dismiss Operation Osprey as a vast publicity stunt, but this is a facile criticism which overlooks the fundamental conservation principle of involving the public in affairs of this sort. It is probably true to say that Operation Osprey would never work at all without the considerable public support it receives—and these days publicity for wildlife and its problems is surely no bad thing. The Scottish Wildlife Trust have certainly supported RSPB

views in this direction, running an excellent and valuable operation of their own at their Loch of the Lowes reserve in Perthshire where ospreys have now become established as breeding birds.

Nor must we overlook the value to naturalists themselves of the weeks that many hundreds of them have spent helping to protect ospreys and to show them to the public. Few of them will forget the excitement of night watches, the beauties of dawn over the reserve, and the incomparable wildlife and scenery of the region. More than that, many of them probably gained their first insight into conservation and protection problems through this kind of direct personal involvement. Even the hours spent diligently writing up the log books in the forward blind have had more value than merely keeping wardens occupied. From the observations of hundreds of helpers we have a more complete idea of the home-life of a pair of ospreys than has ever been obtained before and a scientific analysis was published in 1976.

To go back to the birds themselves—a great deal has happened since the establishment of the Loch Garten pair. While they (and their successors) have used the same site for eighteen successive seasons, the total population has built up to such an extent that the osprey can really be regarded as a fully re-established species, even though it is still confined to the Scottish Highlands as a breeding bird. Protec-

Breeding Record of Ospreys in Scotland

	Pairs Breeding	Successful	Young Reared
1954	1	1	2
1955	1	0	0
1956	1	0	0
1957	0	0	0
1958	1	0	0
1959	1	1	3
1960	1	1	2
1961	1	1	3
1962	1	1	1
1963	2	0	0
1964	2	1	3
1965	2	1	1
1966	2	0	0
1967	3	2	5
1968	3	2	5
1969	4	3	6
1970	6	3	8
1971	7	5	11
1972	12	6	14
1973	13	10	21
1974	14	10	21
1975	9+	7	16
1976	14	10	20

Scottish osprey (left) about to land at nesting tree. Despite constant observation by wardens and widespread public interest in the Loch Garten ospreys, the nest tree was sawn through by vandals in 1964 and the eggs were taken one night in 1971 from under the wardens' noses

Nearly a million people have visited the RSPB's osprey reserve (right, all three pictures), which has resulted in greater support for wildlife conservation in general. The bottom photograph shows wardens erecting protective devices on the nest tree, ranging from electronic warning devices to coils of barbed wire around the trunk

tion measures have been concentrated around the Loch Garten birds and these have borne the brunt of public observation, although in recent years those at the Loch of the Lowes have shared the load. Other pairs have been looked after on a private basis, or hardly at all, with secrecy regarding their whereabouts providing their main protection.

A second pair began nesting attempts in Speyside in 1963 and were back again in subsequent years, shifting to a wholly new site from 1966, but theirs is a long history of successive failures, mostly due to their eggs not hatching. The third pair, this time outside Speyside, arrived in 1966 and first bred the following year, by which time a fourth pair was known, but not yet breeding, again outside the Spey valley. The first year in which two nests produced young was 1967. The spread of the osprey has continued ever since, so that by 1976, some 14 sites were known to be occupied, with 10 successful pairs rearing a total of 20 young. Including the birds reared in 1954, we know that at least 148 young have fledged from Scottish nests since recolonization began.

Sightings of banded ospreys at sites used in the mid-1960s showed that new colonists were still coming from the Scandinavian population, but we still knew almost nothing about the fate of Scottish-reared birds. It was not until 1967 that a banding program was started, but within a few years it was already producing results. By 1972, 44 young had been banded and as many as 7 had already been found dead—killed by man in some cases—6 of them on migration through Spain, Portugal, and western Africa. If the first battle—to protect the new colonists and allowing them to gain a firm foothold in Britain once again—has been won, the second—to ensure their safety once they have left British shores—has scarcely begun. No better illustration could be found to show the importance of international cooperation in the protection of migratory birds.

Banded Scottish ospreys have now been seen with nests of their own, so that we can now say with some confidence that our new population is at least partly self-sustaining. I think we can expect to see their numbers increase to some degree in the years to come. One thing is certain: continued protection of these fine birds is still as important as it ever was and so are efforts to use some of them to enlist still more public support for conservation.

NEW HOPE FOR THE WHOOPING CRANE

by Ken and Marilyn Poertner

The proverb 'birds of a feather flock together' will not, one hopes, hold true for the sandhill cranes of Grays Lake National Wildlife Refuge, Idaho, and their whooping crane foster chicks. Cooperation between the Canadian Wildlife Service, the US Fish and Wildlife Service, the University of Idaho, and the Idaho Department of Fish and Game, has resulted in a unique experiment which may strengthen the survival prospects of the severely endangered whooping crane.

If successful, the project will establish a second population of whooping cranes in the wild, outside the migratory range of the present flock. This existing flock, which numbers about sixty birds, nests at Wood Buffalo National Park in Canada's Northwest Territories; it migrates some 2600 miles to spend the winter at Aransas National Wildlife Refuge on the Gulf coast of Texas. The aim of the joint project is to shorten this route by 1800 miles for the second wild flock, if it can be established in Idaho. The ever-present danger of losing the entire wild population of whooping cranes to disease, storms, oil spills, or other disasters will be greatly reduced by the existence of two flocks.

The experiment stems from the enthusiasm and persistence of one man, Dr Rod Drewien, now a biologist with the University of Idaho Wildlife Cooperative Research Unit. Drewien came to Idaho in 1969 to study the greater sandhill crane and was intrigued by a suggestion first made by Fred Bard of the Regina (Saskatchewan) Provincial Museum of Natural History in the mid-1950s. This concerned the possibility of using sandhill cranes as foster parents for whooping cranes—and in 1972 Drewien submitted a proposal for just such an experiment

Sandhill cranes share many behavioral patterns with whooping cranes and it is hoped that young whoopers can be fostered by sandhills. The object is to build up a second flock of the rare whooping cranes

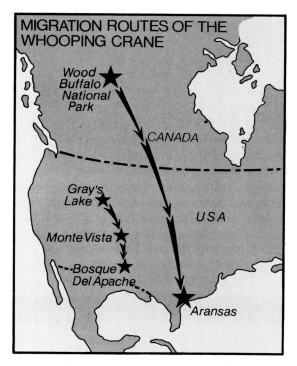

MIGRATION ROUTES OF THE WHOOPING CRANE

Sandhill cranes in flight (above and right): the cranes chosen for the experiment migrate annually between Grays Lake in Idaho and Bosque del Apache refuge in New Mexico, a distance of about 800 miles. The young whoopers integrated well with the sandhills at the wintering grounds even though both species are aggressive

to the US Endangered Species Office.

The male whooping crane reaches a height of up to 5 feet with a wingspread of 7 feet, making it the tallest bird in North America. Sandhill cranes are only slightly smaller. Whooping cranes are whiter and have a more massive bill than the sandhills; they are also distinguished by black-tipped wings.

The two species have many behavioral similarities. Both mate for life, and require a territory of some 30 to 40 acres in which to nest and raise their young. Whooping cranes always nest in aquatic areas, as do sandhills for the most part. They return to the same nesting grounds each spring, to within 1½ acres of the same spot. If they lose a nesting area through the intervention of man they will not seek another location. Both species maintain strong family groups.

Both crane species will battle fiercely to defend their nesting territories, and are very aggressive. Males and females share the incubation of the eggs, of which only two are normally laid each year. Incubation begins as soon as the first egg is laid.

The eggs themselves are almost identical. There is an average of only 1mm difference in size, and although the coloring is very slightly different this is not readily detected by the sandhill cranes.

Whooping cranes, however, have always been known to reproduce poorly. Both eggs usually hatch, but one of the two chicks almost always dies due to sibling rivalry and competition for food. Some biologists believe that removal of one of the two eggs from the nest actually increases the number of chicks to survive each year.

Grays Lake National Wildlife Refuge in Soda Springs, Idaho, is one of the largest nesting grounds for sandhill cranes. It is a high altitude marsh (at 6400 feet) measuring 9 miles by 4 miles and surrounded by fields of grain. Banding of the sandhill cranes and study of their migratory routes has been conducted at Grays Lake for many years by the Idaho Cooperative Wildlife Research Unit.

The US Fish and Wildlife Service carefully selected the potential sandhill crane foster parents, based on banding data and observations of marked birds. Crane pairs that showed a strong tendency to spend the winter at Bosque del Apache National Wildlife Refuge in New Mexico were chosen because both Bosque del Apache and Grays Lake can provide a high degree of safety for the birds. The migratory route between the two refuges is about 800 miles.

After carefully analysing the project's chances of success, the various agencies finally took the plunge in 1975. They gambled 14 of the 31 whooping crane eggs laid that spring in Wood

Buffalo National Park.

Rod Drewien flew in the helicopter with the Canadian scientists who located the nest sites and removed the eggs. If a nest contained only one egg it was left undisturbed. Each egg that was removed was numbered to identify the territory in which it was collected. The biologists used heavy woollen socks to transport the eggs back to their helicopter. From the socks, the eggs were transferred to well-insulated and padded carrying cases where the temperature was carefully monitored. The whooping crane eggs had already been incubated for three weeks by the time they were collected.

Separated into two packages, the whooping crane eggs were flown to Idaho Falls, then taken to the refuge area. Careful records were kept of which numbered egg was placed in which sandhill crane nest.

Then began a period of watchful waiting for the whooping cranes to hatch. The Canadian Wildlife Service kept in close telephone contact with the biologists at Grays Lake. Whenever they observed a new chick near one of their nests they would notify Grays Lake so that a check could be made of the correspondingly numbered egg. Of the 14 eggs transferred, 9 eventually hatched—and of these 9, 6 whooping cranes lived to begin the winter migration to New Mexico.

The young chicks were watched at a distance from birth until they were about sixty days old. They were then banded and color-marked to indicate their origin at Grays Lake Refuge. At ninety days old the young cranes can fly, and begin to gather in flocks for migration. The whooping crane chicks left with their foster parents between 2 October and 22 October 1975. Their route south took them through Monte Vista Refuge in Colorado, then to Bosque del Apache.

Each year between 10,000 and 12,000 sandhill cranes from the Rocky Mountains spend the winter at Bosque del Apache. It was thus a considerable challenge to find the immature whooping cranes among this vast assemblage.

Despite the difficulty, four were located. Two were found at Bosque del Apache, one at Belen State Game Refuge, and one at a nearby farm. The other two whoopers were never seen and are believed to have perished on the journey south.

The immature whooping cranes integrated well with the sandhills at the wintering grounds, even though both species are aggressive. At first some sandhills attempted to attack the whiter whooping cranes. But the foster parents defended their chicks when this happened, and the larger size of the whoopers soon proved to their advantage so that such contests became infrequent.

The same marshy roosting and feeding areas in fields served both whoopers and sandhills. The birds fed mainly on corn and to a lesser extent on alfalfa. They were occasionally seen feeding in aquatic areas. Because the main whooping crane flock is heavily dependent on seafood while it winters at Aransas National Wildlife Refuge, some biologists had felt it might be necessary to fly food supplies from Aransas to Bosque del Apache every week. Fortunately, however, the young whoopers were satisfied with the more prosaic fare available to them at Bosque del Apache.

Strict precautions were taken to protect the immature birds from hunters and predators throughout the winter. The birds were under almost constant observation. Since winter hunting is permitted in some places near Bosque del Apache, each time one of the whooping cranes took flight a horn was sounded warning hunters to hold their fire. This was in addition to many notices that were put up saying that the whooping cranes were in the area and describing their appearance. No harm came to the four young birds during their first winter.

The return flight of the sandhill crane flocks began in early February 1976. All four of the young whoopers were seen at Monte Vista National Wildlife Refuge with their foster parents, resting on the return flight to Grays Lake. But the sandhills rejected the juvenile birds before reaching Grays Lake. This is a natural process with the sandhills, which enables them to start a new nesting cycle.

In late May 1976 the four whooping cranes were still at Monte Vista, apparently with no intention of flying on to Grays Lake. It had been hoped that the return migration would have been completed before the young birds

suffered the normal rejection by their foster parents.

The whooping cranes had to adjust to being on their own through the spring and summer. But assuming this has happened successfully, wildlife biologists are hopeful that by the time the cranes mature sexually in four or five years, they will return to Grays Lake for breeding purposes. There is no easy method of sexing whooping cranes at a distance, but of the four first-year survivors it appears that two are male and two female. It is expected that in due course they will select whooping crane mates, rather than sandhills. In addition to the plumage and size differences already mentioned, the two species' mating calls and ritual 'dances' are also different. A female of one species would very likely be unresponsive to courting by a male of the other species. But in the event of such a pairing taking place, the birds will be removed from the wild flock so that hybrid chicks will not be produced.

The fostering experiment will be under constant evaluation and is planned to continue until 1981. The project is dependent on the nesting success of the main whooping crane flock at Wood Buffalo National Park, and the Canadian Wildlife Service will decide how many eggs can be allocated to Grays Lake each year. In May 1976 a further fifteen whooping crane eggs were taken to Grays Lake and placed in sandhill crane nests; three of these were destroyed by coyotes early in June.

Two lessons learned in the first year should help increase the young whoopers' survival rate in 1976 and subsequent years. The whooping crane chicks proved less skilful than sandhill crane chicks at getting through the cattle fences which crossed the refuge, and the whoopers were much more nervous of cattle grazing nearby. So in 1976 the cattle fences were taken down, and nesting sites farther away from the cattle grazing areas selected for placing the eggs.

Hopes are high that the long-range experiment will succeed in establishing a second wild flock of whooping cranes. Although the future for the whooping crane has never looked rosier, the only certainty is the need for continued intervention by man.

Stop Press

After this article was written it was learned that coyotes at Grays Lake had destroyed twenty-six

Whooping cranes: the present flock numbers about sixty birds and migrates a distance of 2600 miles from Canada's Northwest Territories to Aransas National Wildlife Refuge on the Gulf coast of Texas

sandhill crane nests, including four whooping crane eggs transplanted earlier from Wood Buffalo National Park. Eleven whooping cranes hatched. Of this number, five perished through storms and starvation, one from pneumonia, and one from unknown causes. Four whooping cranes have survived from the 1976 project year, making a total of eight birds fostered by this experiment. Biologists were aware of the location of two of the four whooping cranes surviving from the 1975 project: one was near Grays Lake with a group of juvenile sandhills, and one was alone in Utah. An increased coyote control effort was begun at Grays Lake, in anticipation of the spring 1977 transplant project.

POACHERS VERSUS PARROTS IN AUSTRALIA

by Hans Beste

The majority of the fifty-five species of parrot found on the Australian mainland and in Tasmania are quite common, and although numbers of individuals fluctuate greatly, particularly with those parrots found mainly in the dry interior of the continent (depending on whether the 'center' is in the grip of a prolonged drought or not), there is little concern for the survival of most of them. None of the parrots which use typical nesting sites are threatened, either by bird-catchers or by the destruction of their habitat. A typical nest is made in the hollow of a tree trunk, inside a hollow limb, or in the cavity of a wooden fencepost. There is no shortage of hollows in most open forests, or in the predominantly eucalypt-lined water courses of the inland regions, and as the majority of nesting sites are high above the ground, only a small number are ever detected, even by a keen observer, thus ensuring a high breeding success. Most parrots lay from two to five eggs per clutch, and this, combined with the nomadic nature of many of the inland species, is a further advantage in the parrots' battle for survival.

However, not all parrots have typical nests, and it is these whose existence is now threatened. The mere positioning of the nests has made them vulnerable to man's ways of urban control, or his greed for financial gain. The swamp parrot is one of the species now rapidly disappearing from its former haunts along the south-east coast and the southern fringes of Western Australia as well as Tasmania. A medium-sized, predominantly green parrot, this bird prefers coastal heathlands, estuarine flats, and swamp plains. The nest is made in a thick grass tussock, and this largely terrestrial parrot is rarely seen unless flushed by accident.

The golden-shouldered parrot (this one is a male) is highly prized by collectors, but unfortunately it does not breed well in captivity, leading to a demand for wild-caught birds. This species is also known as an 'anthill' parrot, which is actually incorrect as it nests in termite mounds, not anthills

Due to continuous clearing of its preferred habitat, usually for beach building sites, and only too frequent burning by irresponsible people to keep down the growth—which is considered a high fire danger—the swamp parrot is no longer an easy bird to see on the mainland. It is certainly true that heathland represents a severe fire risk if not burnt from time to time, and controlled burning every few years would even benefit the swamp parrot. It will soon move out of an area if growth is allowed to go on unchecked, but annual burning, now so prevalent in Australia, gives the country little chance to recover. Even before the white man came to Australia, the aborigines regularly burnt the country to drive out game, and lightning ignited many fires, but a more regular and more widely spaced cycle of burning and regrowth made for a better habitat and gave the smaller trees such as dwarf eucalypts and acacias a chance for survival.

A much rarer species, not unlike the swamp parrot, is the night parrot, which was once found throughout the inland areas of every mainland state. A mainly yellowish-green parrot, it can be readily distinguished from the swamp parrot by its very much shorter tail, lack of red patch above the bill, and its preference for spinifex (*Triodea*) type habitat. Once collected regularly from Western Australia, the Northern Territory, South Australia, Victoria, and the south-west corners of Queensland and New South Wales, its preferred habitat appears to have been rocky outcrops and along the margins of salt lakes and samphire flats. No reliable observations of the night parrot have been made for over fifty years, and the apparent disappearance of this ground-frequenting, nocturnal parrot is a mystery to ornithologists. In areas where foxes and domestic cats have spread since the advent of the white man, such predators could be held to blame—but large areas of the inland, covered mainly with spinifex, are far too inhospitable to be infiltrated by these alien creatures. It is unlikely that the night parrot is yet extinct, as rumors of sightings by night truckdrivers, especially in the north-west, cannot be completely discounted. There are reports of green quail-like creatures and green parrots hit by cars at night forthcoming from people in the Hammersley and Kimberley Ranges of Western Australia, when questioned by naturalists. But unfortunately no evidence has so far been presented to confirm these stories.

Few naturalists ever travel in these far-away areas as the country is rather desolate and inhospitable, due to its dryness and the high temperatures which prevail for most of the year. Most travellers pass through this region fairly quickly and few would be tempted to stay and search for the night parrot in an area which is so vast that even a well organized expedition would probably be doomed to failure. Re-discovery of this lost species is thus left to chance. It is hoped that through education, people who do travel through the outback may one day recognize this interesting parrot. This does not only apply to the night parrot, but to many other species which have been lost since the early days of exploration. Travel by camel and horseback left much idle time, which gave explorers many opportunities to seek out interesting new specimens of flora and fauna; indeed, they made it their business to collect anything that could be new to science, which, besides finding new routes, was one of the main reasons for sending out expeditions.

The species discussed so far are endangered mainly because of the changing nature of Australia's countryside, and are not directly persecuted by man. But the disappearance of two other species, known as the anthill parrots, members of the *Psephotus* group, can be directly attributed to man's activities. These birds, much prized by collectors, nest in termite mounds, or termitaria, incorrectly called 'ant hills' by people of the outback of Australia. The two species are represented by three races, with the best known, the golden-shouldered parrot, found on the Cape York Peninsula of north Queensland, and its cousin, the hooded parrot, confined to eastern Arnhemland in the Northern Territory. The second species is the paradise parrot, once found in the now rather densely settled areas of south-eastern Queensland and adjacent New South Wales, but today probably extinct, or certainly beyond recovery.

This species has not been reliably reported since the late 1920s, although rumors have it that two clutches of eggs were collected in 1975. However, the rumors may well have been spread by the person reportedly responsible for the collecting, just as reports of the bird's continued existence were circulated a few years ago when a mutation of two other parrot species yielded birds vaguely similar to the paradise

Female golden-shouldered parrot at her nest-hole in a termite mound. The birds only nest in the mounds of the aptly named magnetic termite (the mounds are generally orientated north-south) and so are easy to find

parrot, and for which a market apparently had to be created. These crosses were offered as the genuine article, but whether anybody was fooled or not cannot be ascertained.

The paradise parrot male was a magnificent bird, with a pale brown back, vermilion shoulder patch and abdomen, and bluish-green neck, chest, and rump. It had a black cap, pale bluish feet and bill, and a light eye ring. The female was a paler edition of the male, with a predominantly blue front, a whitish face, and a green tail. Open savanna forest and grasslands, studded with terrestrial termite mounds, were its habitat. Museum specimens of this parrot show that it was once found in areas which are now suburbs of Brisbane, the capital of Queensland, and although much similar habitat still exists today, it is most unlikely that the paradise parrot will be rediscovered in any numbers; if at all. Whether man is entirely responsible for its demise is difficult to say so many years after its apparent disappearance, as the bird might already have been a vanishing species when white settlers moved into its range—but there is no doubt that its final decline was considerably speeded up by collection. The termitaria, used by the bird for nesting, are only a few feet high, and locating freshly excavated hollows and subsequently digging out the young was comparatively easy for the early settlers. Few of these had any compassion for the local fauna and anything that could be exploited, chopped down, shot, or got rid of in any way, was treated in just that fashion. Sadly, attitudes have changed little since then.

Australia is a vast continent, almost the size of the United States, but with most of its population of $13\frac{1}{2}$ million living on the eastern and southern fringes of the mainland the greatest part is sparsely populated. Except for Perth, the capital of Western Australia, and a few isolated towns here and there, including Alice Springs in the center of the country, the remaining area has a population density well below one person per square mile. Few good roads lead through the 'outback', and anybody who wants to 'rough it' or feel like an early pioneer certainly has no trouble finding isolation away from settled areas. This also applies to the law-breakers, however, and especially those intent on illegal bird and wildlife trapping. The lack of concern shown by the general public, and the arrogant attitude of many people, who make it their sport to slaughter anything that presents itself during a weekend hunting trip, aids the culprits. Law enforcement is pathetically inadequate, with police officers normally having to patrol huge areas, and wildlife offenses being treated as of little importance.

It is therefore not surprising that although most bird species are protected by law, very few professional bird catchers need fear being apprehended or prosecuted. Most parrot species (as well as finches) are in great demand by aviculturists, especially overseas, and as there is a complete ban on the export of all native fauna from Australia, illegal trapping is the only way to satisfy the call for new stock.

Most species of parrots which are prized by collectors breed readily in captivity, and so the demand for wild-caught birds is not as great as it is for those which are difficult to breed. Unfortunately, however, Australia's most prized bird, the golden-shouldered parrot, falls into the latter category. If it was a matter of providing nesting boxes for the bird to breed, there would not be a constant demand for new birds caught in the wild to replace captive birds as they die, or to cater for a growing market. The golden-shouldered parrot and the hooded parrot are only bred rarely, obviously not taking too easily to hollow logs or boxes as substitutes for termite mounds, and this has resulted in extensive bird smuggling of these species from their breeding ground to the more densely settled areas, but particularly to the overseas market.

The Cape York Peninsula has many large land holdings, used almost exclusively to graze cattle, and except for the bauxite mining town of Weipa on the Gulf of Carpentaria, there are no towns of any size within its boundaries. Some properties (known as stations) are well in excess of 1000 square miles in area and may not support more than one family and a number of stockmen, as cowboys are called in Australia. One dwelling and a few sheds may be the only buildings on such a property and most of the stockmen, who are usually aborigines, sleep under the stars for most of the year. The Cape is mostly savanna woodland, dissected by a few large rivers and many creeks, which only run in the wet season, numerous water-lily lagoons, and a few rocky ranges in which rainforest gullies may be found. Most creek-beds are fringed by monsoonal belts of

deciduous trees, and these harbor the greatest concentration of wildlife.

Many of the savanna areas are in low-lying flood plains, often covered with great numbers of termite mounds; but only one type of mound, built by the magnetic termite, is used by the golden-shouldered parrot for its nesting site. The termite gets its popular name from the general north–south configuration of the roughly wedge-shaped mound it sometimes constructs. However, many outrunners are built in all directions from the main structure, and a completed mound is anything but regular in shape. This type of mound is usually found on the fringe of a plain, but because it is not particularly thick it is rarely successfully excavated by the golden-shouldered parrot.

Partly dug tunnels can often be found in these termitaria, but it is a second type of mound, built by the same species of termite, that is generally preferred and successfully used by the parrot. This structure is rather thicker, being shaped like a cone or witch's hat, and can be up to fifty centimeters in diameter at the base, narrowing to a point at the top. This gives the bird almost unlimited possibilities for excavating a nesting chamber, and many mounds display a series of tunnels, one above the other, showing that it has been used year after year.

By the middle of April the wet season, which floods the Peninsula with torrential rain from January to March each year, is almost over. Only a few occasional showers now refresh the lush green growth which has sprung up everywhere since the floodplains have started to dry up. Termite mounds are relatively soft at this time, carrying more moisture than usual, which makes digging much easier. The pair of golden-shouldered parrots which used the mound last year is still together, and has decided to use the same mound again this season, but a new nesting chamber has to be excavated as the termites closed the old hole up again after the last breeding season.

Hanging on to the mound's surface with its strongly clawed feet, the parrot chips away at the mound with its beak. Bit by bit the dark gray soil breaks away, but the bird soon tires and its partner takes over. Constantly changing over, the pair soon make a small hole in the mound and as their foothold becomes less precarious, the time that each bird spends at work lengthens. The parrots only dig a few shifts each day at first, but as they progress and the

Gould's drawing of the night parrot, once found throughout Australia, but not reliably seen for fifty years. The apparent disappearance of this ground-frequenting nocturnal parrot is something of a mystery, and it is not impossible that it will be rediscovered

tunnel deepens, they work longer hours. The time for egg-laying is approaching and driving the birds on to work even harder. By the end of April the nesting chamber is complete. A tunnel runs for eight to ten inches horizontally into the mound, just wide enough to allow the parrot to crawl through. The nesting chamber at the end of the tunnel is much broader, and large enough to hold the incubating bird and four or five white eggs. As the parrots excavate the nesting chamber, they lay bare a great number of tunnels used by the termites to move about, but these are quickly blocked up by the hosts and the nest soon becomes completely isolated from the activities of the termites.

When the young birds hatch, some two and a half weeks later, they are fed inside the mound by their parents until they are ready to leave the nest and—one hopes—before the mound is located by a bird-collector.

When white men first came to Australia, more than two hundred years ago, the golden-shouldered parrot was quite common, and like many other, predominantly grass-seed-eating parrots, it could be found in flocks roaming the savannas of the Cape York Peninsula. This

situation didn't change for a long time, as the area was almost inaccessible and the hooded parrot was safe just as long as the tracks leading into the Northern Territory remained in their rough state. However, during World War II, a major road was built by the United States Army to link Alice Springs with Darwin, to facilitate the rapid movement of troops. This road led right through the center of the hooded parrot's range. Similar improvements, although the road was not bituminized, made the track into Cape York (and through the golden-shouldered parrot's territory) an access artery for the cattle properties that were then being developed.

A great number of bridges now span the rivers of the Cape and the advent of the four-wheel-drive vehicle eventually opened up the last few rough areas of both breeding ranges. The bird-trappers became even better equipped as they ferried out their booty—and as they made more money. Light planes soon flew loads of golden-shouldered parrots out of the Cape. When all export of native fauna was banned, fast boats took the catch out of the country, and this still happens today. Although there are fewer parrots leaving Australia, the

79

price that they bring is much higher. An almost total lack of coastal patrols encouraged the smugglers and a complete absence of wildlife rangers in the Cape made the whole operation easier. The point has now been reached where most cars, including conventional sedans, can reach the breeding grounds of the golden-shouldered parrot, and although the species is now totally protected and there is now one ranger responsible for the Cape York Peninsula, the bird has become so rare that it is almost impossible to find, even in areas where many excavated termite mounds and dug-out nests stand as silent reminders that the species lived in the area only a few years ago. Gone are the days when flocks of these magnificent parrots could be seen feeding on the seeds of fresh green grass; only a few isolated pockets, with just a handful of birds in each, survive. However, given a chance, the golden-shouldered parrot could make a come-back. The habitat is still intact, the birds lay a good clutch—usually five eggs—and all that would be needed for its recovery is law enforcement and keeping bird-smugglers out of the area.

The property owners and managers are not really interested in the bird's survival, and those who know of its value are more often than not responsible for illegal trafficking themselves; they helped many of the collectors in the past and probably still do so today. Stockmen are certainly happy to be given A$5 per chick, and are known to have collected great numbers.

The law is almost helpless where big money is involved, and the two police officers stationed in the Cape have far more important things to do than trying to catch bird thieves. The ranger, who was appointed as recently as 1972, has to patrol the entire area, some 400 miles in length and over 250 miles in width, and deal with everything relating to the wildlife protection laws. This means that he has to try to stop not only the catching of golden-shouldered parrots, but also the catching of finches, numerous other parrots (especially in Iron Range on the east coast, where several New Guinea species occur), and try to curtail the plundering of native orchids, the catching of pythons and lizards, the illegal shooting of crocodiles, and many more such activities.

Birds are usually smuggled out of the country in a drugged state, but a large number appear to die well before reaching their destination, judging from reports which come from time to time from the customs department. The only way to stop the trafficking is to stop collecting.

Fortunately, the hooded parrot is not yet in the same predicament as the golden-shouldered parrot, although it is still collected illegally. Several small towns in the Northern Territory are well within the species' range, and the local police officers have been well briefed on the potential bird smugglers. With the help of local magistrates and a few heavy sentences in the past, they appear to be keeping the situation under control. This species differs from the golden-shouldered parrot in that the male lacks a yellow spot above the bill, having a larger yellow shoulder patch, and a smaller red abdominal patch. The female lacks the pale cap of the golden-shouldered parrot. The species is also found in flood-plain country, but uses round, pudding-shaped termite mounds, made by a different type of termite. These mounds are usually yellow or ocher in color, depending on the soil type.

What then can be done to ensure that the golden-shouldered parrot and the other threatened species survive? Obviously all trapping of wild birds must be stopped, and although laws forbid trapping, this fact alone has not been enough in the past and is not likely to succeed in the future. Ideally, the demand for these birds should be reduced and although the Australian Government could make it an offense to keep the threatened species, it would be most unlikely to persuade foreign governments to follow suit. Therefore, much stricter control and enforcement of laws, as well as higher penalties for offenders, appears to be the only answer.

The swamp parrot would be safe in its habitat if burning was controlled and if no further breeding areas were allowed to be subdivided. With the coming of compulsory environmental impact studies in most areas, the future of this species looks far brighter than that of the other endangered parrots, especially as it is found in the more populated south-east, where people are far more aware of conservation issues, and where any plans for large-scale clearing are fought hard by conservationists. Several areas have already been set aside as national parks and fauna reserves to protect the swamp parrot and for the time being it is holding its own.

The night parrot and paradise parrots, however, cannot be protected until their status and

The hooded parrot is also much sought after, like its close relative the golden-shouldered parrot, but is not in quite such a bad state. It also nests in termite mounds, but termites of a different species

possible distribution is more clearly known. The golden-shouldered parrot is thus the main species upon which conservation efforts must be concentrated. The majority of people living in the area are not interested in conservation, and this applies to the whole of northern Queensland and the Northern Territory, as is evident from the wholesale plunder of fauna and flora, which is allowed to go on almost unchecked. Fines, if imposed, are generally inadequate, and there are so many loopholes in the law that prosecution of offenders is rare. It seems ridiculous to impose a fine of a few hundred dollars on a person when the haul of birds with which he is caught would have a potential market value of many thousands of dollars. Even if his equipment were to be confiscated as well, another successful trip would soon pay for the loss.

The major problem is the lack of manpower in the breeding range of the bird, and particularly during the breeding season. It would probably be much more effective, therefore, to station at least one ranger permanently in the area, and have another two rangers patrol the breeding range during the breeding season from May to June, when the young are in the nests and the species is thus most vulnerable to collecting. That this method would be successful can be seen by the continued existence of good flocks of hooded parrots near towns in the Northern Territory where police officers are stationed. It would not cost the government a great deal of money to supply the necessary rangers and station them in the breeding territory of the golden-shouldered parrot. Although there are policemen in the Cape York Peninsula at Laura and Coen, the birds do not really breed on their doorstep. Enforcers of the law are just too far away to be effective in preventing bird-smugglers from entering the areas without being detected.

If the golden-shouldered parrot is to survive for posterity, steps to ensure its protection will have to be taken now. Delay could be disastrous, and this beautiful bird could easily follow the paradise parrot down the road from which there is no return.

MANAGING THE PRIBILOF FUR SEAL

by Erwin Bauer

In 1784, the American vessel *States* arrived in its home port of Boston with a most unusual cargo: 13,000 fur seal pelts from the faraway Falkland Islands. Few Bostonians then had ever even heard of the Falklands or of fur seals, but soon the golden skins proved to be almost worth their weight in real gold and a frantic world-wide race began to obtain more of them.

During the next five decades, fur seal rookeries so numerous in the Southern Hemisphere —Juan Hernandez, the South Shetlands, Mas-a-fuero, Prince Edward, the Antipodes, and countless other lonely islands—were destroyed as fast as they were discovered. New England and British skippers hauled many millions of pelts to Chinese markets where they were traded for silk, tea, and other products of the Orient. By the beginning of the nineteenth Century, the only fur seals clinging to a precarious toehold on earth were pitifully small herds on coastal islands off South Africa, New Zealand, and in the Galapagos.

It is difficult to say exactly what effects these events and discoveries had on Imperial Russia, except that as an emerging world power, they certainly spurred the Czar to quickly find fur sources of his own. Russian explorers and seafarers in the New World had already noted the migration each spring of huge numbers of fur seals in the Unimak and other narrow passes through the Aleutian Islands. But once beyond there the mammals just seemed to evaporate into the Bering Sea.

Among those officers most determined to follow the seals to their ancestral breeding ground was one Captain-Commander Gerasim Pribilof. He sensed there would be fame and fortune waiting for whoever found it, but knew it would be a difficult task in a part of the world where foul weather never seemed to end.

No written record remains of the day in 1786 (or maybe 1787) that somebody aboard Pribilof's boat sighted land. No doubt the sudden presence of masses of seabirds alerted the Russian that land was within reach. Probably the steep cliffs and tundra-covered extinct cinder cones were first glimpsed at dangerously close range, and just intermittently through thick fog and mists. Perhaps Pribilof approached near enough to one of the two islands now named after him, to hear seal bulls bellowing well before he could see the outline of rocky beaches. But no matter; what was probably the largest fur seal rookery of all time had been discovered at last.

What followed was exactly what the reader will suspect. Exploitation of the Pribilof herd followed the same destructive pattern as that pursued by sealers at the opposite end of the globe. Aleuts were moved by Russian boats to the previously uninhabited islands to harvest the seals (females and pups included), the kill being limited only by how fast and efficiently they could kill and collect. By about 1834 the population had been all but wiped out, as earlier had the sea otters and walruses. After that, fearful of losing the revenue and not from conscience, the Russians belatedly banned the killing of females. But from the time of Pribilof's first beachhead until Alaska was sold to the United States in 1867, a minimum of three million pelts were taken.

Even after the sale of Alaska, the survival of

Uncontrolled slaughter reduced the fur seal population of the Pribilof Islands almost to extinction by the middle of the nineteenth century. Now, however, the hunt is carefully managed and the great herds thrive again

northern fur seals hovered in grave doubt. Killing continued, largely unregulated, for many years. The first complete census made in 1912 revealed only 215,900 animals and it was not until international agreements were signed in 1911 and 1957 that the future of fur seals of the entire northern Pacific was guaranteed. For their own profit, Russia, Japan, Canada, and the United States agreed that the animals should be managed on a scientific basis, that there should be no pelagic hunting (that is while the animals are migrating at sea), and that profits of the harvest should be shared by all. The harvest is now being managed each summer on the Pribilofs by the US Department of Commerce. And now the huge total of 1½ million fur seals return every year to the two main islands, St George and St Paul.

But exactly what is the northern fur seal, *Callorhinus ursinus?* A widely ranging mammal with 30 million years of experience in navigating open oceans, it is seldom seen alive except by commercial fishermen from Alaska southward to the Oregon coast, or by visitors to the Pribilofs and certain Asian islands where the seals gather in summertime. Besides St Paul, St George, and Sea Lion Rock of the Pribilofs, the animals also breed on Copper and Bering islands of the Commanders off Kamchatka, on Robben Island off Sakhalin, and on Kotikoviya and Srednevoya islands in the Kuriles. Fur seals had been exterminated from the latter two places by about 1890, but reappeared in small numbers in the 1950s. Yet 80 per cent of *all* northern fur seals are from the Pribilof Islands.

A young German, Georg Wilhelm Steller, was the first European to describe the species. During dusk of August 10, 1741, while taking part in an exploration voyage to mainland Alaska, he observed a 'sea ape' swimming near the ship and noted it in his journal. While shipwrecked the following summer on Bering Island, he watched astonished as the same 'sea apes' came ashore to breed. But it was not until after the 37-year-old naturalist's death that publication (in 1751) of his *De Bestiis Marinis* introduced the fur seal to science and the western world. Among the facts Steller did not discover was that a fur seal pelt contains 300,000 hairs per square inch, making it exceedingly rich and luxurious.

Today the pelts taken from the Pribilofs alone are worth more than $6 million a year, which is almost as much as the United States

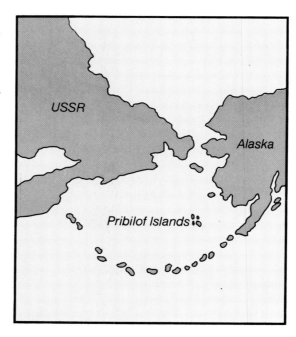

originally paid for the entire 49th State! Even in these times of inflation it explains (but does not justify) why men have murdered one another for the luxurious coats and why politicians of more than one country have pandered to the profit made from skinning far too many animals for the species' own good.

Nowadays it is possible for a tourist, either with a strong taste for offbeat places, or greater than average curiosity about the natural world, to see both the Pribilof Islands and fur seals on a very intimate basis. At least twice a week throughout the summer, Reeve Aleutian Airways makes scheduled flights from Anchorage via Cold Bay to St Paul. During the summer of 1974—188 years or so after Pribilof—my wife Peggy and I made the trip. Considering world events in between, we found surprisingly little change from what the Russian navigator must have seen.

Even for the most sophisticated ocean travellers, the sight of massed, mating fur seals is something quite extraordinary. Nowhere else in North America (except possibly at Carlsbad Cavern in New Mexico, during the evening exodus of bats) is it possible to stand in one place and see so many mammals at any one time—or to find so many focused in the viewfinder of a camera. Certain of the major rookery beaches seethe with life, the thousands of fur coats seeming velvety from a distance. And in early July the fur seals are not just lolling in the comparative warmth of a brief Alaskan sum-

Sealers and whalers have in the past been inclined to slaughter their quarry even more relentlessly than other exploiters of wildlife. But luckily the process was stopped in time on the Pribilof Islands, and the fur seals are now managed on a strictly scientific basis

mer. There is constant activity, some of it violent, accompanied by a constant din of bellowing, croaking, and roaring, added to which is an all pervasive animal odor which might be described as fishy.

By the first of July the beachmasters or harem bulls have been ashore for at least a month and the mightiest, dominant ones (which arrived first) have already established themselves in the best possible places to acquire cows. Some of the most powerful manage harems of 25 or 30 and occasionally even more. These they defend and keep segregated in a knot from other lesser bulls which have had to freelance or to take less strategic beach sites. Here and there sits a bull with only one or two cows, plus another bull waiting to move in.

As long as there are any females still to come into oestrus, there is conflict, with battle-scarred bulls trying to move in on another's property.

Savage fights occur, and blood squirts from new wounds on the swollen necks of antagonists. But at the same time, small and silky black pups of 10 or 12 pounds are being born to most cows. Shortly after the birth, the cows mate again. That is a curious sight, too, because at about a quarter of a ton or more, males weigh five times as much as the females.

Mortality of the pups in those super-crowded rookeries is very high. The life is suddenly squeezed out of many as copulating adults roll over on top of them. We also saw one bull, which had finished second in an encounter with a beachmaster bull, taking out his frustration on a nearby pup. He grabbed the pitiful young one by the throat, shook it as a bulldog shakes a rat, and tossed it high into the air, continuing in his aggression long after it was dead. A short time later one of the numerous foxes of St Paul appeared on the scene to drag the carcass away to a nearby den.

Most tourists to the island are restricted to visiting only one or two of the rookeries (one from a weather-proof stone blind). There are several reasons for this: some beaches located on distant, remote parts of the island are not easily accessible by bus; also it is a safety measure—in the past some foolish camera-toting travellers went too close to lovesick bulls and landed themselves in serious trouble. But mostly this confinement of tourists to certain spots is meant to allow the summer harvest of seals to proceed unobserved and unimpeded.

On a typical day during the July sealing season, a crew of 20 to 50 experienced Aleut sealers will surround a large herd and try to block its escape to the sea. Three and four-year-old bulls are separated as much as possible, then driven to an open area on the tundra. There all male animals of desired size and good pelage are quickly dispatched by clubbers with a single blow on the head by a hardwood pole. Obviously this method of killing is the subject of great controversy and many other ways have been tested, but clubbing remains the quickest and most efficient. Each year a total of about 50,000 young males are taken in this way from the Pribilof rookeries. This figure is considered to be the annual surplus which is safe to harvest. At least during the past decade or so the northern fur seal population has been maintaining itself at the same high level, which is probably the maximum for the environment.

A good many of the growing number of visitors to St Paul nowadays are interested in more than just an intimate glimpse of a fascinating ocean mammal. For sheer spectacle, here also is one of the finest mixed seabird rookeries anywhere. Most such colonies from the Bering Sea to Baffin Island contain one or two, or maybe three, species of birds nesting at any one time. Here we counted a dozen. For the record, our list includes common and thick-billed murres; black- and red-legged kittiwakes; horned and tufted puffins; least, paroquet, and crested auklets; pelagic and red-faced cormorants; and fulmars—all of these together on the face of one cliff along the western shore of St Paul.

Even more noteworthy than the galaxy of seabirds is the ease with which their rookery may be reached. In a career devoted largely to wandering around the world to hunt wildlife with a camera, I can recall no similar place so

Beachmaster bull fur seal (above) on St Paul Island. A male weighs about a quarter of a ton, and is thus five times as heavy as a female fur seal (top left). The large bull (left) in the centre of the picture is surrounded by his harem. Some of the biggest bulls will acquire harems of twenty or thirty cows, which they defend zealously from other bulls. Savage fights occur, and often the baby seals are rolled on and killed in the melee

conveniently accessible by public transport, and where so many species can be observed simply by crawling out towards the crest of a cliff. In some spots even that is not necessary to watch the never-ending comings and goings of birds busy with housekeeping and feeding chicks, perched on the edge of apparent eternity.

In one place Peggy spotted a pair of puffins sitting on a rock about 300 feet directly above an angry gray surf. To get as close as possible for pictures, I crawled infantry-style on my belly to the very edge. Then, looking straight down, I stared with amazement right into the face of an equally astonished Arctic blue fox. How any four-footed animal without wings ever reached that thin ledge is more than I can explain. Apparently it had mastered cliff climbing and was living on seabird eggs and chicks.

Despite the ease of access, it is possible on a typical day, while sitting atop a bird cliff, to believe you are marooned on the loneliest island on earth. A north-west wind whines against cracks and crevices. Low clouds come drifting in at water level, totally obscuring any view of the ocean, and isolating you on a small tundra island where even the cries of the seabirds so near by sound muted and faraway.

Today the human population of the Pribilofs is about 480, most being engaged in the summer sealing with an increasing number in catering for tourists. Both of these occupations are very seasonal and brief, and unfortunately both come at the same time. The Aleuts of St Paul are housed in one village of fairly snug clapboard and plywood homes, lined up as geometrically as similar dwellings in Burbank.

Flying back to Anchorage, with any last look at the Pribilofs probably blanked out by a soupy overcast, a passenger has a chance to reflect on what he saw on one of America's remotest ocean outposts. This will surely include the wild-flower 'show' which is incredibly beautiful and long to be remembered. Vast areas of lupine and lousewort, of moss campion, heather, primrose and avens, many unique to the Pribilofs, brighten the haunting beauty of St Paul during the endless days of midsummer. But maybe it is the seal harvest that, at least for a while, occupies most of one's thoughts.

It is true that the northern fur seal is doing well—it would be gratifying indeed if all the world's endangered species were doing half as well. But can we justify the killing just to furnish fur coats for a few of the world's wealthiest people? Is providing a livelihood for a few native people a sufficient rationale? In these days of expanding international tourism—and a growing concern about wildlife—would this remarkable ocean resource be worth more as a tourist attraction than as a giant fur farm? Would the Pribilofs be a vastly more valuable natural asset as a national park, or even an international park since the fur seals also spend part of their lives in waters off Canada, Japan and the Soviet Union?

All are questions we will have to answer some day—and perhaps very soon.

VANISHING FISH STOCKS

by Tony Loftas

The world fish catch now stands at about 70 million tonnes (77 million tons) per annum. Apart from a sharp fall in 1972, following the failure of the Peruvian anchoveta fishery, the world catch has held steady or increased every year since 1945. The world catch of fish used directly for human food, rather than for the production of fish meal and oil, has increased every year, although the rate of increase has faltered in recent years. The potential catch of conventional food fish is estimated to be about 120 million tonnes, but could be as high as 200 million tonnes. If species that are now largely or wholly unexploited, such as oceanic squid and lantern fish, are included, the total could exceed 200 million tonnes and might be as high as 450 million tonnes. The potential yield from one unconventional resource alone, the krill of the Southern Ocean, could be 150 million tonnes per year and is unlikely to be less than 50 million tonnes.

Despite such encouraging estimates of the world's potential resources, the fact remains that many fish stocks, rather than making a sustained annual contribution to world catches, are being depleted at an alarming rate. Recent growth in the world catch has become increasingly a measure of the extent to which the development of new fisheries, particularly in sub-tropical and tropical areas, has outpaced the decline of traditional fisheries, especially those in the northern waters of the Atlantic and Pacific oceans.

Few fish species are thought to be threatened with extinction. The 1972 Convention on International Trade in Endangered Species of Wild Fauna and Flora, for example, lists twenty-three species of which only eight are considered to be in real danger. Several of the listed species are relics of an evolutionary past, such as lung-fishes and the coelocanth. The list could easily grow if the collection of ornamental fish for aquaria continues to expand. For the most part, however, the changing fortunes of exploited fish populations are marked by a rise and fall in fisheries dependent on them. Local extinctions may occur as a result of over-fishing, or populations of one species may be so weakened that other opportunist species displace them. Occasionally, sudden environmental changes combine with the direct effects of fishing to cause a catastrophic reduction in a fish population.

Overfishing is not a recent phenomenon. Almost the first historical records of fisheries refer to the decline in yield from one fishery to another. It has come strongly to the fore in recent times because of the continuing expansion of the world fishing fleet and the great catching power of modern vessels. In the past the effects of overfishing have been cushioned by moving on to new stocks. But within a decade from now all major fish stocks will probably be known and exploited. This and the poor results of international efforts to regulate fisheries have helped persuade many coastal nations to claim the living resources lying off their shores. By 1977, for example, all countries bordering on the North Atlantic will have established 200-mile fishing limits. However, it has yet to be seen whether they will prove effective in conserving commercial fish stocks.

Every ocean has its share of fully exploited or depleted fish stocks. In general, the level of exploitation is highest in the northern hemisphere—the first home of the commercial fleets of Europe, North America, and Japan. As with most generalizations, important exceptions exist. An interesting exception from the northern hemisphere must be the discovery of large stocks of blue whiting in the waters north-west of the United Kingdom. The stocks which at present are only marginally exploited have a potential annual yield of more than one million tonnes. The outstanding example from the southern hemisphere must be Peru's anchoveta fishery. Once the largest single species fishery in the world with a catch exceeding 10 million tonnes, adverse environmental conditions and overfishing brought it crashing to a halt in 1972. Since then the fishery has begun to recover, but even in 1976 the total catch was unlikely to reach 5 million tonnes.

Herring trawler in the Inner Hebrides. The herring stocks of the north-east Atlantic are on the verge of collapse, after the fishing catch reached a record level in 1974

Krill—until recently the food of baleen whales—is now being harvested directly by man. The potential yield could be 150 million tonnes a year, or about twice the present world fish catch

CAPE FLATTERY HALIBUT FISHERY
(Canadian and US catches)
— in metric tonnes per annum

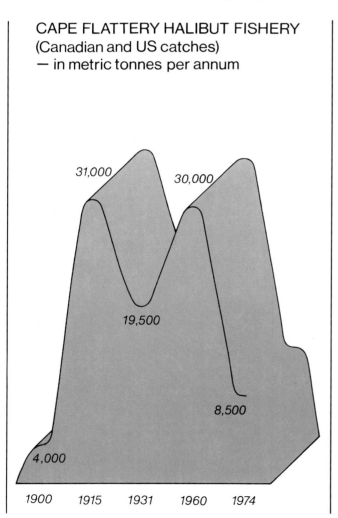

31,000   30,000

19,500

8,500

4,000

1900   1915   1931   1960   1974

TOP TEN FISHING NATIONS
Average catch 1968−72
in thousand tonnes

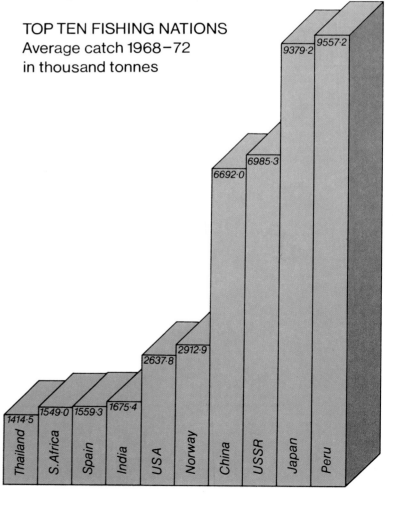

Thailand	S.Africa	Spain	India	USA	Norway	China	USSR	Japan	Peru
1414·5	1549·0	1559·3	1675·4	2637·8	2912·9	6692·0	6985·3	9379·2	9557·2

WORLD FISH CATCH

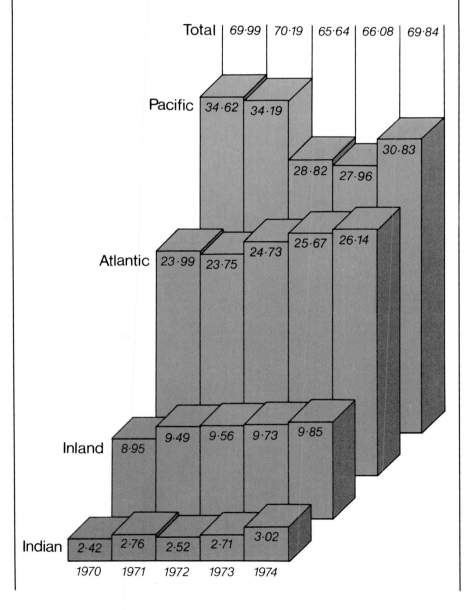

	1970	1971	1972	1973	1974
Total	69·99	70·19	65·64	66·08	69·84
Pacific	34·62	34·19	28·82	27·96	30·83
Atlantic	23·99	23·75	24·73	25·67	26·14
Inland	8·95	9·49	9·56	9·73	9·85
Indian	2·42	2·76	2·52	2·71	3·02

The Pacific Ocean, which covers nearly a third of the earth's surface, provides about half of the world marine fish catch. Among the stocks believed to be either fully exploited or depleted are the large tunas, salmon, Alaska pollack, hake, halibut, anchoveta, and sardines. Many of its fisheries are dominated by the roving fleets of Japan, the Soviet Union, and, more recently, the Republic of Korea. New national fisheries have developed or are still developing in the region, some of them at a startling rate. For instance, Thailand's total catch increased seven-fold between 1960 and 1970. But there are signs that this growth has come to a halt and that some fisheries such as those in the Gulf of Thailand are beginning to pay the penalty of heavy exploitation. Just what the penalty can be is shown by the sardine fishery in the eastern central region of the Pacific. The potential of the stock which is exploited by Mexico and the United States is down to 20,000 tonnes. If the stocks could have been maintained at the high level occurring around 1930, an annual yield of 470,000 tonnes should have been possible.

The Atlantic Ocean, which is about half the size of the Pacific, is the most heavily fished and productive of the oceans, and in 1974 it yielded only 4 million tonnes less than the Pacific Ocean. It also has some of the most serious overfishing problems. Most, if not all, of the major stocks are either fully or over-exploited. In the north-west Atlantic, the total catch has remained at around 4 million tonnes since 1966, despite increasing effort and exploitation of previously unfished stocks such as mackerel, hake, and capelin. In the north-east Atlantic where the catch reached a record 11.8 million tonnes in 1974, the herring stocks are on the verge of collapse. The menhaden, which accounts for almost three-fifths of the fish caught in the western central Atlantic, is now fully exploited. In the eastern central Atlantic, most of the easily accessible or caught fish are fully exploited and some, for example the small surface shoaling sardinellas, may well be overfished.

The Indian Ocean is still considered to be a growth area even for conventional species although most of the coastal resources of shrimp and other high value species such as the large tunas are probably fully exploited. The problem is to know the present levels of exploitation and the precise nature of the catches in this region. Nearly half of the catch from the eastern Indian Ocean, for example, is reported as consisting of 'miscellaneous marine fishes' to the Food and Agriculture Organization of the United Nations, which compiles world fishery statistics. In the western Indian Ocean, little data exists on the total fishing effort. Thus predictions of the untapped potential of the Indian Ocean as a whole tend to rest less on the analysis of existing exploitation than on theoretical considerations of the biological productivity of what is still a poorly understood ocean.

The Southern or Antarctic Ocean is even less well understood although already some stocks have been depleted by heavy fishing. The prime example of over-exploitation in this ocean, however, does not relate to fish but to marine mammals, particularly the large baleen whales. In fact, the hunting of Antarctic whales to the brink of extinction accounts at least in part for the large potential crop of krill. This small prawn-like crustacean forms the principle diet of the blue whale. Prior to the start of whaling, the whales consumed an estimated 180 million tonnes of krill each year as compared with about 30 million tonnes now.

One of the most startling examples of overfishing is that of the herring stocks off Iceland and Norway and, more recently, in the North Sea. The herring stocks lie within the area which, since 1954, has been regulated by the North East Atlantic Fisheries Commission (NEAFC). The Commission, like many of the other twenty or so multinational regulatory bodies, is essentially a political body: each commissioner works in the best interest of his national fishing industry. Since 1964, NEAFC has referred scientific problems to the Intergovernmental Council for the Exploration of the Seas (ICES) which was established as long ago as 1902 to assist European fishery development. Unfortunately there has been a conflict between political wills and scientific advice. In 1974, for example, the Commission responded to signs of overfishing by reducing the total allowable catch of North Sea herring from 550,000 tonnes per year to 488,000 tonnes. This quota was still well above a limit of 390,000 tonnes recommended by ICES. An attempt to slash the quota the following year to a mere 169,000 tonnes met with objections but eventually in October 1975, temporary agreement was reached on a quota equivalent to an annual catch of 174,000 tonnes. A year later the United Kingdom banned herring fishing in its waters for the rest of the year.

Many international fishery commissions can be accused of doing too little too late, but they cannot always control the destiny of fish stocks. The International Pacific Halibut Commission is a case in point. The Canadian and American halibut fishery off Cape Flattery, Washington, began in 1888. Uncontrolled, the catch increased from some 4000 tonnes at the turn of the century to nearly 31,000 tonnes in 1915. Thereafter the catches began to decline and despite greater fishing effort had fallen to a little over 19,500 tonnes by 1931. A joint commission, later to become the IPHC, was established in 1923. By the early 1960s catches of halibut, the largest of the flatfishes, had been restored to a level of around 30,000 tonnes. Unfortunately, a decade later its fortunes had been reversed again. This time the problem is not overfishing by the halibut fishermen but the removal of large numbers of juvenile halibut by other fisheries, particularly Soviet and Japanese trawl fisheries. By 1974 the total catch of Canada and the United States had fallen to less than 8500 tonnes.

High levels of capture of young fish, this time by deliberate fishing, have helped to create a strange situation in the fishery for the Atlantic bluefin tuna—a fish that lives as long as twenty years and can attain weights in excess of 300 kilograms. The catch has declined from a peak of about 40,000 tonnes in 1964 to 16,000 tonnes in 1974. The decline has been greatest in catches of large fish. The Norwegian purse seine fishery, which once took 10,000 tons, has practically disappeared and catches by the Mediterranean trap fisheries are now very low. Those large fish that are caught tend to be heavier and older in successive years. Medium-sized fish are almost completely absent. Large catches of small fish, combined (it seems) with a high death rate among young fish, are preventing the tuna from surviving much beyond five years. The fisheries for large bluefin tuna are therefore relying largely on generations of fish born before heavy exploitation of young fish began in the late 1960s.

Over eighty-five per cent of the world catch comes from the sea. Most examples of vanishing stocks therefore come from the marine fisheries, but the problem is by no means restricted to them. Pollution takes a heavy toll

Chinstrap penguins stand guard over the carcasses of fin whales lying astern a factory ship. This photograph was in fact taken on the last expedition of the last British factory ship. Sustained worldwide protests and boycotts have combined with economic factors to force most nations out of the whaling business

in freshwater fisheries, as is evidenced by those of Lake Erie in North America, but resource depletion through overfishing still occurs. The ningu once occurred in great numbers in the shallow inshore waters of Lake Victoria in East Africa, and associated rivers. During the 'rains' the mature fish would move up the rivers to breed, passing a barrier of nets and basket traps on the way. The future of the fishery depended greatly on the number of spawners that successfully ran this gauntlet. From 1935 to 1951, the fishery and catches remained stable, but between 1951 and 1963 efficient floating gill nets were introduced and the numbers of barriers and traps increased. The catches began to fall. Small populations of the fish still survive in the rivers and some smoked ningu is still sold seasonally at local markets, but the once flourishing fishery is no more.

Finally, some thought ought to be given to the wide range of species, both freshwater and marine, that feature in home aquaria. Ornamental fish have become big business: the retail value of the trade, including accessories, is an estimated US $4000 million world-wide. Ornamental fish form an important export item in many developing countries and this is very much a growth industry. The eastern Asian countries which dominate the market breed and cultivate a large proportion of the fish that they sell. Fish which do not breed in

captivity must inevitably be taken from wild stocks. The brightly colored fish that abound in the East African rift lakes, for example, have become increasingly popular. Most species are restricted to specific lakes which have become isolated nests of evolution. Over-zealous collection of these species could easily lead to their extinction. Similarly, several of the coral fish featured in saltwater aquaria, which these days are quite easy to maintain, are in danger of over-exploitation. The popular clown or anemone fish has practically disappeared from beach areas in East Africa where collectors have traditionally operated. They are abundant only on the remoter offshore reefs.

Despite the long history of the fishing industry, most living resources in seas, lakes, and rivers are either unmanaged or mismanaged. Because of this a substantial part of the aquatic harvest is wasted, and in a few cases the very survival of a species may be threatened. The fishing industry is the only major food producing system in the world that still relies largely on hunting, exploits wild stocks, and harvests animals many of which may be considered common property. Man's influence on the fish populations is exerted almost entirely through exploitation. Furthermore, where stocks are available to all comers, the build-up of fishing tends to be checked only by the cost of each new addition to the fleet set against the value of its catch. In this competitive situation, each country tries to secure the largest possible share of the total yield. The stage is set for overfishing. The basic aim—to harvest the excess production of nature over that needed to maintain the stock at its most productive level—is lost somewhere in the melée.

The future of the world's fish stocks depends not on ownership as such but on the relationship between management and scientific advice. Short-term interests have tended to outweigh longer-term or international interests in the fishery commissions. The tendency has proved greatest where scientific advice has been uncertain, conflicting, or inconclusive. The trend in fisheries management is now towards economic control through the allocation of catch quotas rather than reacting to disaster or a threat of overfishing. But, as in fisheries as far apart as the Pacific halibut and the North Sea herring, quota systems and other regulations can still fail, particularly where scientific advice is ignored or other fisheries intrude on the stocks.

The extension of fishing limits are less important than the objectives of individual governments at the national level for fisheries totally within their jurisdiction, or at the international level in the case of multinational fisheries. In some fishery commissions the body that provides the scientific advice is separate from the political body. In others, the same delegates that eventually make management decisions bring the resource information together.

Whatever the future mechanisms of control may be (and the days of some fishery commissions seem numbered), accurate assessments of the state of fish stocks and the potential outcome of regulatory measures will be needed. The conservation of healthy stocks and the restoration of depleted ones will rest on the quality of management decisions and the ability to enforce them. Even when only one country is involved the great catching power of modern fleets, plus the need to operate them efficiently, can soon cause the fishery, if not the species on which it is based, to vanish.

With catches of conventional fish falling, British fisheries experts are urgently looking into the possibility of using deepwater fish as a source of food. The redfish *Trachyscorpia* (right) is pleasantly flavored and keeps well. On the other hand, the smooth-head (below right) is very sloppy in texture, with a water content of over ninety per cent and less than half the protein of other fish

THE NARWHAL THE STRANGEST CETACEAN

by Randall Reeves

The cetacean order ranges from the gigantic, filter-feeding rorquals to the smaller, unobtrusive porpoises, but the narwhal, a medium-sized species found exclusively in cold Arctic waters, is in some ways the most intriguing cetacean of all. It even has a place in folk lore—the male narwhal's magnificent, twisted tusk was for many centuries said to be living proof of the existence of the illusory unicorn.

Thanks to the remoteness and harshness of its habitat, the narwhal has been largely ignored by modern science. Both its relatively low oil yield, and its elusiveness, have enabled the narwhal to avoid the destructive attention of most commercial whaling fleets. As a result our ignorance about its habits, abundance and distribution, and its life history, is profound.

Ten years ago Fred Bruemmer, a Canadian photographer and writer, described the netting of narwhals in Koluktoo Bay by Canadian scientists who were seeking to answer some basic questions about narwhal biology. Arthur Mansfield of the Canadian Fisheries Research Board, who organized that effort, finally published his results in 1975.

Between 1963 and 1965 Dr Mansfield's technicians measured and dissected sixty-two netted narwhals. Examination of pregnant specimens revealed fetuses between twenty and thirty centimeters long, and two newborn calves were caught. These data, together with information provided by Fred Bruemmer on narwhal calves and fetuses in north-west Greenland, have led Dr Mansfield to hypothesize a mid-April rutting season and a fifteen-month gestation period. These figures correspond closely to those for the beluga or white whale, another Arctic species whose biology is much better known than that of the narwhal. It is likely that female

Very little is known about the narwhal, an inhabitant of Arctic waters and probably the strangest of all cetaceans. Its tusk was long associated with the unicorn legend, but its purpose is probably as a secondary sexual characteristic, rather like a man's beard

narwhals, like belugas, attain sexual maturity at about five years of age and that they give birth to a single calf every three years.

The practical effect of Dr Mansfield's early conclusions was the institution in 1971 of an annual limit of five killed narwhals per Eskimo hunter in the Canadian Arctic. However, he admits that if every potential hunter caught his quota in a given year, the Eskimos of Canada's Eastern Arctic could legally kill up to 1500 narwhals. He adds that if one takes into account the number of animals killed but not recovered, this could result in a kill more than three times the annual production of a narwhal population estimated at around 10,000 animals.

In order to refine estimates of the narwhal population and to monitor native exploitation, a new research effort was launched by the Fisheries Research Board in summer 1975. David Sergeant, head of the project, sent technicians to two settlements in the High Arctic: Pond Inlet and Arctic Bay, both at the northern tip of Baffin Island. He kindly allowed me to tag along with Bill Doidge and Rick Adams who, with the indispensable help of David Ipirq, Arctic Bay's premier narwhal hunter, hoped to measure and dissect narwhals killed along the shores of Admiralty Inlet.

The narwhal apparently derives its common name from the old Norse word 'nar' which means corpse. It has been said that inspiration for the word 'narwhal(e)' came from the animal's piebald, whitish appearance which it acquires with age. Dr Mansfield says the name refers to the presumed likeness of its mottled skin to that of a drowned man. Certain behavioral observations made during the hunt led Bill, Rick and myself to speculate further on the intriguing subject of narwhal nomenclature.

During the open-water period, roughly mid-July to mid-September, the men of Arctic Bay hunt narwhals in outboard-driven freight canoes. The usual technique for capturing these whales is to drive them into the shallows, where they are shot with rifles and allowed to drift ashore. There they are skinned (*mattak* is an Eskimo delicacy) and their tusks (in the case of males and an occasional tusked female) removed. Ten years ago narwhal ivory, most of which is sold to the Hudson's Bay Company, fetched $1.25 a pound; in 1975 the going rate was $30–35 a pound.

The herding principle used by the hunters to force narwhals close to shore is facilitated by the tendency of the whales to swim ventral-up (on their backs) while being chased. Even very old narwhals have enough gray blotching on their dorsal sides to provide good camouflage against the gravel substrate and the greenish-blue of the water itself. However, at an early age the belly of the narwhal begins to whiten, and individuals with tusks several feet long have all-white ventral sides. If the narwhals were to remain upright while fleeing from the canoes, they would be very difficult to spot and track underwater. But in the characteristic ventral-up position, which the animals invariably assume and maintain during the chase, they remind one of ghost-like torpedoes—or moving corpses—their pale bellies contrasting sharply with the dark background.

The family Monodontidae includes two relatively primitive whale species: *Monodon monoceros*, the narwhal, and *Delphinapterus leucas*, the beluga. Both have unfused cervical vertebrae, and they are in fact the only whales able to bend their necks to a considerable extent. Observations of captive belugas in the New York Aquarium suggest that this anomalous anatomical feature is particularly useful to a whale swimming ventral-up when it wishes to maintain a visual fix on an above-water image. Belugas in aquaria, particularly males, are known to spend substantial periods 'resting' on their backs. The extent to which this behavior is an adaptation to captivity, where much of the activity experienced by the whale is initiated from above, is not known.

I once watched a wounded narwhal floating on its back about fifteen yards from shore in Arctic Bay. It drifted, motionless, about eighteen inches below the surface for perhaps five minutes. There were no canoes in the immediate vicinity, and it was not being chased. If it was looking at anything, it was probably at those of us humans who were watching from the shore. When the whale finally surfaced to breathe, it resumed a dorsal-up posture.

Ventral-up swimming, or resting, probably serves a visual function, although this assumption has not been proved. It might also provide some kind of hydrodynamic advantage—for more relaxed flotation or improved swimming proficiency. An acoustic explanation has been suggested for upside-down swimming by other cetaceans, and sound transmission or sound reception may have something to do with this behavior on the part of narwhals. In any case, it seems likely that the narwhal was dubbed the corpse whale by someone who had seen it swimming, for whatever reason, on its back, looking for all the world like a torpedo-shaped ghost.

Narwhals and belugas, along with the sixty-foot Greenland or bowhead whale, are the only cetaceans adapted to spend their entire lives in the ice-infested waters of the far north. While man is without doubt the narwhal's most destructive enemy, at least four other animals can be regarded as occasional predators on narwhals.

Killer whales or orcas are known to eat small cetaceans and pinnipeds when the opportunity presents itself. Eskimos in Arctic Bay attribute much of the near-shore and in-shore movements of the narwhal to the presence of killer whales. However, orcas are not often observed in Admiralty Inlet. According to records of the Royal Canadian Mounted Police, killer whales drove narwhals onto the beach at Pangnirtung, south-east Baffin Island, in 1962 (80–100 narwhals) and 1963 (33). Ipirq, our guide, told me that in August 1959 killers chased ashore 41 narwhals in Admiralty Inlet. Apparently this incident was not reported, since it is not reflected in RCMP records.

Ipirq also told of a dead killer whale that he examined near the southern tip of Admiralty Inlet. The animal's head had been impaled by something that entered the mouth and exited somewhere on the side of the head. He assumed, judging from the angle and shape of the wound that it was made by a narwhal tusk. There are no known reports of narwhals employing their tusks in defense against predators, although some old accounts by whalers suggest that narwhals ram boats with their twisted, tapering tooth. Burn Murdoch, in *Modern Whaling and Bear Hunting* (1917), remarked 'we might have had his great ivory tusk through our boat, as has happened before. They have driven their spear though many inches of an oaken keel. You can see such a keel in Bergen Museum.'

Most speculation about uses of the tusk includes the possibility of its employment as a fencing implement, an ice pick, a spear for capturing fish, and a prod for stirring up bottom-dwelling prey. But many scientists today regard it as little more than a secondary sex character, similar to a cock's comb or a man's beard. Few would defend its utility as a weapon.

Perhaps the most interesting in a long line of theories about uses of the tusk is the acoustic jousting proposition advanced by Peter Beamish, a Canadian bio-acoustician. Robin Best, a graduate student at the University of Guelph (Ontario), reported having felt strong vibrations in the tusk of a captured narwhal as the animal vocalized underwater. This observation prompted Dr Beamish to speculate about the use of the tusk as an acoustic wave guide. Tusked bulls could square off head-to-head and transmit intense, piercing sounds, radiating principally off the tips of their tusks. The narwhal with the longer tusk would be able to place the sound source—that is, the anterior end of its tusk—nearer the sensitive ears of its adversary, thereby driving it from the area with ear-splitting sound waves. Longer tusks, then, would have a selective advantage, since normally the winning jouster would successfully mate with the female or females at issue. Dr Beamish is anxious to test his ingenious theory with live narwhals.

In addition to killer whales, walruses are thought to be an occasional threat to narwhals. Although these great tusked pinnipeds seem to prefer shellfish as food, they are known to prey on seals and whales when molluscs and crustaceans are not available. Richard Perry, in *The World of the Walrus*, summarizes numerous nineteenth-century records of walruses attacking and devouring narwhals. The most dramatic of these is an account by the English whaler Robert Gray, whose father in 1879 described an encounter between an adult narwhal and a walrus. His ship came upon the scene moments after the narwhal (a 14-footer with a 5-foot tusk) had been dispatched by the 11-foot walrus. Gray speculated that the narwhal had been subdued in the following manner:

The only way I can think of is that he (the walrus) had found the narwhal asleep, gone underneath him, dug his tusks into his belly, and clasped him around the body with his flippers, in which position we found them, with this difference, that the walrus was uppermost.

Walruses are extremely rare in Admiralty Inlet, and the Atlantic walrus population in general is much reduced from earlier times. Their scarcity, coupled with their apparent preference for mussels, whelks, clams, and

Female narwhal (left) breaking surface in a north Greenland fjord

crabs, make walruses unlikely enemies of the narwhal, especially in this part of the Arctic.

Polar bears roam the Arctic in search of seals, and their great strength enables them to kill an odd whale from time to time. Degerbol and Freuchen, in their *Report of the Fifth Thule Expedition*, published in 1935, assert that 'a small flock of bears will congregate and kill a small whale, which they will then drag up on the ice and eat.' Just as they manage to grab ringed seals, their principal prey, with powerful front paws while lying on the ice, polar bears sometimes have the opportunity to kill belugas and narwhals in a similar manner. While I did not personally witness any attempts by bears to catch whales, the Eskimos of Arctic Bay recognize the polar bear as a narwhal predator.

A nasty gouge in the dorsal side of one female narwhal shot by the Eskimos may well have been made by a hungry bear. The published accounts of polar bears catching and eating beluga whales are sufficient to establish, by inference, the strong likelihood that narwhals, too, are occasional victims of these aggressive predators.

Finally, Greenland sharks certainly relish narwahl skin and blubber. In some parts of the Arctic these 'sluggish carrion grummers', as Bruemmer refers to them, are quite common. While the Arctic Bay Eskimos are certainly familiar with sharks, I saw but one during six weeks in Admiralty Inlet. This 9-footer, high and dry on the beach, had a stomach full of *mattak* (narwhal skin) that it had barely begun to digest.

In lower latitudes sharks are known to prey on dolphins, but it is not clear whether Greenland sharks successfully attack either narwhals or belugas. It is certainly conceivable that narwhals are sometimes caught napping unwarily at the surface and bitten by these scavengers. But no doubt most narwhals eaten by sharks have been killed and lost by Eskimos or by another of the narwhal's natural enemies.

Attempts to capture and display live narwhals have been disappointing. Murray Newman, Director of the Vancouver Aquarium, led expeditions to Baffin Island in 1968 and 1970. Altogether, six narwhals were taken alive to British Columbia, one of which survived for four months. It was a 9-foot male with a 15-centimeter tusk. The only other effort to maintain a narwhal in captivity was undertaken by the New York Aquarium in 1969. An orphaned calf whose mother had been killed by the Eskimos of Grise Fjord was flown to the Coney Island facility. It survived for a month before succumbing to pneumonia. Very little was learned from the hapless captives, however, since their handlers were understandably

Though man is the major predator on the narwhal, killer whales, walruses, and polar bears all manage to catch the occasional animal. Narwhal ivory now fetches some $35 a pound, compared with $1.25 a decade ago

pre-occupied with trying simply to keep the whales alive.

Perhaps there is a better way to learn about the narwhal's frigid underwater existence. During the past several years great progress has been made by divers trying to penetrate the dark, icy waters of the Canadian North. In August 1973 two divers near Pond Inlet who were searching the ocean floor for artifacts, were approached by a female narwhal that followed them to a depth of about sixty feet. Later they found themselves encircled by a dozen bulls with spiral tusks up to eight feet long. The creatures surrounded them, and viewed them from every angle. A year later they returned to take the first known underwater motion pictures of free-swimming narwhals. The Film Board of Canada had a crew in Koluktoo Bay in 1975, their sole reason for the trip being to

film narwhals underwater. Their labours were largely unrewarded, thanks to Eskimo hunting activity, unco-operative weather, and the narwhal's own unpredictable movements.

As development of the Canadian North proceeds at its dizzying pace, however, there will be many more opportunities to observe and record the habits of narwhals in their native habitat. At the same time, it becomes increasingly important for us to know details about their abundance and life history. The presence of ice-breakers, tankers, and freighters in the Arctic cannot help but affect the life of the sea mammals there. Dr Sergeant, in his work with belugas in Cunningham Inlet west of Baffin Island, found the whales to be immune to quiet terrestrial observation but easily disturbed by waterborne noises, even by a skipped stone. Between the direct efforts of Eskimos to kill narwhals, the disturbances caused by increased ship traffic, and the inevitable contamination of Arctic seas by mining activities, the formerly obscure 'unicorn of the sea' may regretfully soon take its place on the list of endangered species.

THE DESERT PUPFISH FIGHTS FOR SURVIVAL

by Robert Rush Miller

In the deserts of the American Southwest, most notably in the well-below-sea-level, desolate floor of Death Valley, lives a remarkable group of fishes known as pupfishes, members of the genus *Cyprinodon*. Pupfishes occur in a variety of habitats extending from the eastern and southwestern United States into Mexico and southward through the islands of the Caribbean to northern South America. These active little fishes, 25 to 76mm. long, comprise at least twenty-five species, but only nine of them occur outside arid regions.

Because of their remarkable tolerance to highly mineralized and hypersaline waters, and their ability to spawn over a temperature range from about 13 to nearly 40°C, pupfishes are able to survive where other fishes cannot live. In fact, they are uncommon in habitats that are not physiologically demanding. By thus avoiding predation and competition, pupfishes have become uniquely adapted to isolated desert springs, creeks, and pools—some as hot as 47°C. How did these fishes come to inhabit deserts, including the lowest and hottest region in the Western Hemisphere?

During the past million years or so, when glaciers covered much of northern North America, the desert was a well-watered land, containing numerous large and small lakes and connecting river systems. It was then that pupfishes were able to reach their now isolated desert habitats, which are but shrunken remnants of these Ice Age waters. Some of these lakes persisted until only 30,000 years ago or less.

Until quite recently, deserts were largely untouched by man's activities. It was not until the 1950s that a real threat to pupfish survival began to develop as man's growing populations over-

Male Nevada pupfish: a splendid representative of an extraordinary group of fishes that are uniquely adapted to life in deserts, including the lowest and hottest region in the Western Hemisphere

Devils Hole, Death Valley National Monument, Ash Meadows, Nevada: a surface view (left) showing visitors standing on the viewing platform at the far end; and looking up from the water level towards the viewing platform (right). A water level recorder, a bank of lights, and an artificial shelf are in the foreground

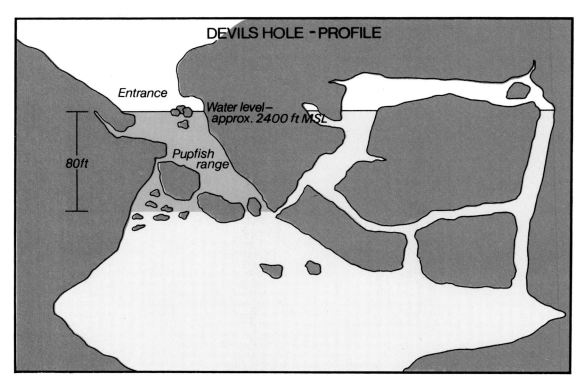

DEVILS HOLE - PROFILE

Entrance

Water level—
approx. 2400 ft MSL

80ft

Pupfish
range

flowed into desert environments. Here he has created an unprecedented demand upon already limited water resources. When I studied pupfishes in the California and Nevada deserts thirty-five to forty years ago, there were but tiny oases of human invasion, but now whole areas are dotted with man's habitations and his cultural accouterments, and the once unbelievably clear desert air is being invaded by smog, which I first noted in Death Valley in 1971. Ecosystems, particularly the fragile isolated ones in deserts, are the products of thousands of years of adaptive evolution and cannot survive rapid, radical environmental disturbance. That desert fishes have persisted in some of these tiny habitats for millennia is an amazing fact in itself.

Until 1969 the name pupfish was virtually unknown to the public—not one in 500,000 Americans had ever heard of it. Since 1970, however, the plight of the pupfish has been widely publicized in national magazines, the news media, and on TV programs that have been seen overseas as well as in the United States. One species in particular, the dwarfed Devils Hole pupfish (whose Latin name, *Cyprinodon diabolis*, is longer than itself!) has attained prominence as a unique and endangered species—officially recognized as such in the IUCN world listing of endangered freshwater fishes and by the US Secretary of the Interior. In 1970, the latter established a Pupfish Task Force to coordinate government efforts for the preservation of pupfishes and their habitats. In that same year, the Desert Fishes Council was formed in order 'to provide for the exchange and transmittal of information on the status, protection, and management of desert fishes and their habitats'.

All pupfishes are charming animals with interesting behavioral traits that have only recently been revealed. They may be easily observed darting about their pools while feeding, 'leapfrogging', pursuing mates, or showing aggressive behavior—especially during the breeding season, which typically lasts for as long as eight months and may be nearly year-long in hot springs. The deep-bodied males are particularly colorful, with iridescent metallic blues and purples on their backs and upper sides, often with black or purplish vertical bars on their sides when courting or fighting, and with black borders on their fins and sometimes yellow on the tail region; their dorsal fins are marked with white, yellow, orange, or pinkish tan. Females are slimmer-bodied and more somber in color, often mottled with tan or greenish brown, and typically have dark vertical bars on their sides.

All pupfishes are gregarious and are opportunistic (omnivorous) feeders, devouring a variety of organisms that are often associated with the typically luxuriant algal growths that pervade their sunlit habitats. They will also feed on aquatic and even flying insects and may consume the dead remains of their own kind. Their playful habits, such as flip-flopping back and forth over floating objects, have earned them their vernacular name.

Most pupfishes live in shallow water, generally not much over a meter or two in depth, and they are frequently active in summer months in water scarcely deeper than their bodies. In freezing weather, they hibernate by burrowing in the soft detritus characteristic of stream-bottom habitats. They can tolerate salinities up to nearly five times that of sea water (to 160 parts per thousand) and they live at elevations varying from more than 200 feet below sea level, on the floor of Death Valley, to 6230 feet above in Durango, Mexico.

A distantly related genus (*Aphanius*) shows convergence because it lives in similar environments about the Mediterranean region and the Near East, including the basin of the Dead Sea, with the result that it has developed habits and general appearance much like *Cyprinodon*; it was once classified in that genus.

In 1952, President Truman withdrew from the public domain a 40-acre tract of desert in Ash Meadows, Nevada, including Devils Hole, as part of Death Valley National Monument, which otherwise lies wholly in California. The proclamation noted the unusual features of Devils Hole and specifically referred to the pupfish, 'a peculiar race of desert fish found nowhere else in the world'. This action was believed to set aside for posterity this unique pool of water and its extraordinary endemic pupfish, *Cyprinodon diabolis*. From that time until very recently, the Devils Hole pupfish was little disturbed by man's activities and continued to live as it had for some 30,000 years previously. Then, in 1965, a ranching corporation moved into Ash Meadows, which at that time contained many beautiful springs in addition to the clear pool in Devils Hole. The company acquired and cleared land, permanently altering many of the aquatic habitats, sank wells, and in 1967 began pumping water out from under the desert for livestock development. As this operation proceeded the water level in Devils Hole began to drop. Thus began a life and death struggle for the Devils Hole pupfish that continues to the present.

Devils Hole is an extraordinary, cave-like habitat, without surface outlet but with constantly changing water from a very deep-seated aquifer. It lies near the base of a black hill in the Ash Meadows desert some 30 airline kilometers east of Death Valley. From the air it is seen as a black chasm in the barren rock some 33 yards long and 10 to 16 yards wide at the surface. Its walls drop nearly vertically for 50 feet on three sides to a 22-yard-long pool of warm, clear blue water, at one end of which is a shallow rock platform about 5 yards long. Along the fourth side, erosion has formed a rough stairway of loose boulders that leads down to the pool's surface. This pool, 2400 feet above sea level, extends deep into the carbonate rock; it has been explored by scuba divers to a depth of nearly 300 feet without finding or seeing bottom. Over a period of almost fifty years, the nearly constant water temperature has varied narrowly between 32.8 and 33.9°C, despite the fact that air temperatures fluctuate annually from about 9 to 45°C. Yet its amazing fish inhabitants, when tested experimentally, were found to have essentially retained the ability of other pupfishes to tolerate a wide temperature range, varying from 5 to 44°C.

Although the surface of Devils Hole is not a true cave, the spring pool provides an environment markedly different from those of the springs and creeks just outside Devils Hole in the adjacent part of Ash Meadows. Unlike those habitats, Devils Hole lacks natural predators for adult fish, contains a great scarcity of food during the winter (when sunlight fails to reach the pool surface for long periods of time), and its uniformly warm temperature eliminates the pupfish option of hibernating that occurs in habitats where there is a normal winter period of food shortage. This latter feature places great stress on the population of Devils Hole pupfish that accounts for the very marked decrease in numbers during the winter season. It is believed that the reason why such predators as aquatic insects, common in outside waters, do not occur in Devils Hole is that the surface pool is not visible to such predators as may fly over it, for only a black gash appears from the air. It has been estimated that under pristine conditions in favorable years (e.g., prior to 1968) the total population of Devils Hole varied between about 300 individuals in late winter to 900 in late summer. By the spring of 1972, however, when this pupfish was first accurately censured, its total population was at least 50 per cent below normal, as its small breeding and nursery area was being threatened by a steadily falling water level that had dropped at least one meter since 1968.

Unlike all other species of *Cyprinodon*, the Devils Hole pupfish is non-territorial; thus males do not set up territories that they guard and defend from all intruders. Loss of territorial behavior in this species probably evolved in response to the very restricted available spawning area on the natural rock ledge at the southern end of Devils Hole; the water level over much of the outer part of this ledge originally varied in depth from about 1 to 3 feet, being very shallow only near its shoreward end. It is on this shelf that the species depends for food, reproduction, and a secure nursery for the young, for it is only here that the water is of proper depth and the bottom (rubble) of appropriate composition for spawning and shelter of young, and only here that sunlight strikes the water surface to stimulate algal growth so vital to the food requirements of *Cyprinodon diabolis*. The species eats chiefly diatoms, amphipods, ostracods, protozoans, and a green alga, in which some of these organisms are enmeshed. The most important part of the natural shelf for young fish, which are about 3 to 5mm. long, is the shallower portion.

If the water level recedes farther, exposing this natural ledge, there are no other such ledges below, upon which the fishes can rely for feeding, breeding, and rearing of young.

Unlike all other pupfish, *Cyprinodon diabolis* also exhibits a pattern of more or less regular, migratory behavior. As determined by underwater observations with scuba gear, most if not all of the population descend daily during many months to a depth of 30 to 50 feet (a few go deeper). No young (3–5mm fish) leave the surface ledge, but juveniles (5–12mm long) have been noted at depths of about 16 feet, and adults (14–30mm long) go farther down—even to 80 feet. This behavior may be in response to the intense solar radiation that floods the shallow surface ledge during part of the day.

Female Cottonball Marsh pupfish. The fish have earned their name because of their playful habits, such as flip-flopping back and forth over floating objects

The Devils Hole pupfish also exhibits a relative fearlessness of man comparable to that of the wildlife in the Galapagos Islands, as noted by Darwin in 1835 during the voyage of the *Beagle*. In addition, compared with other pupfishes, it shows reduced escape responses and the species is definitely less aggressive than others of its genus. This fearlessness of man and the reduced escape responses have probably been important to the survival of *Cyprinodon diabolis* during the periods, especially in recent decades, when considerable disturbance of its limited habitat has occurred during man's activities in Devils Hole. The installation of a water-level recorder by the US Geological Survey, early exploration of the Hole by scuba divers, and, more recently, nearly three years of population censusing to determine the relationship between water level and population size, plus attempts in 1967 to remove and count the entire population, might well have been fatal were it not for the docile nature of this fish. If you move slowly, it is possible to catch by hand juveniles and even adults.

As the underground pumping continued and the water level declined, an artificial shelf made of fibreglass with rubble placed on its surface was installed in May 1970, adjacent to the natural ledge, in an effort to produce more spawning and feeding habitat. Subsequently, artificial lights were placed over this shelf to stimulate algal growth. Very limited success resulted from this manipulation, however, and the shelf was removed in December 1974, with no convincing evidence that it had materially aided the population.

Attempts made over a span of nearly thirty years to propagate the Devils Hole pupfish in both private and public aquaria, in out-of-door ponds, and in natural (fishless) springs have uniformly met with complete failure. Other pupfishes are readily bred in captivity and a few have been successfully transplanted into natural springs. Some factor or factors in the life history of *Cyprinodon diabolis,* in association with its unique habitat, has precluded the successful establishment of this species outside of Devils Hole. Thus survival of this species can be assured only by maintaining its original habitat in a condition satisfactory for its perpetuation. This means that excessive pumping from the Devils Hole aquifer must cease so that normal or satisfactory water levels can become re-established.

A particularly noteworthy effort to establish

this fish in a refugium built especially for it by government agencies at first seemed to indicate success. A special concrete tank was constructed above the Colorado River below Hoover Dam, oriented in the same north-south direction as Devils Hole, supplied by water similar in temperature and water chemistry, stocked with algae, invertebrate animals, and rubble from Devils Hole, and covered with protective screening regulated to admit similar amounts of sunlight. Twenty-four adult *Cyprinodon diabolis* were introduced in October 1972 and by late January 1973 had reproduced to yield a total population of 86 fish. As often happens when fish are stocked in a new habitat without competition from other species or predators, a population explosion took place over the next few years. Despite this increase, scientists were uneasy because of the initial small number of fishes transplanted, which some felt might not contain sufficient genetic variation for long-term success, and apparent changes in the appearance of the offspring born in the new environment. By early 1974, the population seemed to have stabilized at somewhat more than 200 individuals. However, by the summer of 1975, a drastic decline in the stock had set in (possibly due to the highly inbred strain) so that before the end of that year the population had dwindled to only 55 adults. The original fears thus seemed well founded.

In response to the declining water level in Devils Hole, the US Government (Department of the Interior) sought court action for an injunction against unrestricted pumping of ground water and a declaration of ground water rights. From a detailed study of the hydrology of Ash Meadows by the US Geological Survey, that was fostered by the Interior Department's Pupfish Task Force, it is known that three wells in particular affect the water level of Devils Hole. The District Court and Appeals Court in Nevada ruled in favor of the pupfish to the effect that pumping of the ground water was to be restricted so as to maintain a prescribed level in Devils Hole. However, it became questionable whether that level would allow sufficient water coverage over the natural rock shelf to assure long-term survival of the Devils Hole pupfish. Consequently, on January 12, 1976, the US Supreme Court was asked to rule on the ground water rights in Devils Hole. In effect, then, the Supreme Court, for the first time in history, had to decide the fate of an entire species. On June 7, 1976, in a precedent-setting decision, the Court ruled unanimously that when the federal government requires land for public use it obtains rights to both the surface water and groundwater needed to preserve the character of the land, including the wildlife. In effect, this ruling requires that the water level in Devils Hole must be maintained at a level sufficient to assure perpetuity of the species.

Strong efforts have been made and must continue to be made to secure the survival of the Devils Hole pupfish and other threatened species, since they are needed for research to explain how these animals have been able to survive in their fragile and often extreme environments. Their remarkable adaptations create intriguing scientific problems involving comparative physiology, population dynamics, ecology, genetics, behavioral responses, and other disciplines that have important implications to current environmental problems faced by man himself. When desert springs dry up prematurely and the pupfish die, it becomes simply a matter of time until the environment will no longer sustain man.

The female Devils Hole pupfish (right) is slimmer and darker in color than the brilliantly-hued male (below right). This species was first protected by President Truman in 1952, but in 1967 a ranching corporation began pumping water from beneath the desert, which lowered the water level in Devils Hole. Eventually the Supreme Court decided the fate of an entire species when it ruled that the ground water level must be maintained

REPTILES

TORTOISES COME TO BRITAIN

by John A. Burton and Mike Lambert

In British usage tortoises are land animals, turtles marine, and terrapins fresh-water. To add to this confusion, the common terrapin of Europe is usually known as a pond tortoise. The word turtle in general popular usage in the United States applies to all three forms, while the word for tortoise in German is *Schildkröte* (shielded-toad!).

Tortoises—the land animals—have been popular as pets since time immemorial. The ancient Greeks and Romans kept them, and sometimes carried them in their ships as a food supply that could be replaced by rocks or ballast. Many were eaten by the French soldiers of the Foreign Legion, but not by the Algerians who feared them to be evil spirits; the taste of the flesh resembles chicken.

Nearer to our time, the parson-naturalist Gilbert White had a pet tortoise. The habits of Gilbert White's 'Timothy' are recorded in detail in *The Natural History of Selborne* and the shell of the deceased Timothy is preserved in the Natural History Museum in London. Timothy lived to the age of at least 85 years. A record of 102 or 125 years has been given for a tortoise in captivity, depending on whether a tortoise taken to Lambeth Palace, London (where it is preserved) by Laud, Archbishop of Canterbury, in 1633 died in 1730 or 1753. The animal was at Fulham Palace in 1628 when Laud was Bishop of London. Possibly more reliable records are those of 96 and 54 years. However, most tortoises imported into Britain are not so fortunate.

Ever since 1895 tortoises have been imported into Britain commercially. Initially only a few hundred were imported each year. During the early part of this century, the figure rose substantially, into the thousands. They arrived in the Port of London by ship from Casablanca, packed in wicker baskets stowed upright on deck. By 1938 a peak of a quarter million in one year was reached, many of them tiny hatchlings only two or three inches long which had hardly any chance of surviving the cold, damp British climate. World War II brought temporary respite to the tortoises, but by 1949 the trade was in full swing again with hundreds of thousands being brought into Britain each year. This trade has continued, more or less unchecked, right up to the present day (1976). The only concessions that have been made to the tortoises are that they cannot be imported commercially outside the summer months, and the import of baby tortoises has stopped. The latter control could be of a rather dubious value to the survival of wild tortoise populations, since breeding adults are imported instead.

Some export restrictions have been imposed by the Moroccan Government on tortoises dispatched by local dealers from Casablanca. Technically the export of tortoises with an undershell of less than four inches is forbidden. At the same time, larger specimens with an undershell measurement of more than six inches take up a lot of space in the dispatch baskets relative to their size, resulting in a proportionately lower financial return per animal. Moreover, these large specimens are sold less readily by dealers in Britain for they tend to alarm small children. Thus, only about two-thirds of the whole population of tor-

Horsfield's tortoise comes from the dry steppe-lands of Central Asia, and is therefore quite unsuitable for importing into Britain. Yet between 1966 and 1972 an average of 17,000 of this species came in each year. A leading figure in this trade (until apprehended) was a former professor of zoology at the University of Tashkent

(Overleaf) The Mediterranean spur-thighed tortoise sometimes wrongly called the Greek tortoise, comes to Britain mostly from North Africa, especially Morocco. But some may now be coming from Turkey in order to satisfy the demand

toises collected are suitable for export, and dealers also discard badly damaged animals. However, the exporting size range (four to six inches) excludes some small mature males and very large females, in addition to juveniles. It is possible that these animals may continue to breed if left in the wild and not brought by local collectors to Casablanca. But because of the size difference, successful matings are not likely. Many tortoises are dumped on the nearest garbage tip when refused by the dealers.

Apart from a tourist banjo trade which can utilize these 'outsize' tortoises in their manufacture, and the use of baby tortoise shells as souvenirs or scarf toggles, there are few other demands for tortoises outside the pet trade. Evidence suggests that in North Africa the distribution of the tortoises is a relict of a far greater range so that these much diminished populations could be particularly vulnerable to mass exploitation even if still viable with relatively infrequent matings. Thus, extinction could result if the chances of males meeting females for breeding purposes become remote.

In all, nine or so species of tortoises are imported commercially into Britain. They all belong to the genus *Testudo* and include *T. pardalis*, *T. elegans*, *T. sulcata*, *T. elongata*, *T. carbonaria*, *T. marginata*, *T. graeca*, *T. hermanni* and *T. horsfieldii*. Of these it is the last four which cause particular concern. They are found in Europe, North Africa, and the Near East. With the exception of *T. marginata* they have formed the bulk of the pet tortoise trade in recent years. Since 1965, when the Animals (Restriction of Importation) Act 1964 became fully operative, statistics have been published each year. These give the numbers of tortoises licensed for import (prior to 1965 licences were not needed) and the table summarizes the imports.

Testudo marginata, the marginated tortoise, is one of Europe's rarest reptiles. It is confined to a limited part of Greece, though colonies also exist on Sardinia and Sicily where they were probably introduced by Greek settlers or sailors, or even monks, many centuries ago. In appearance the marginated tortoise superficially resembles *T. graeca* and when young is very like *T. hermanni*, but with age a noticeable flare develops to the rear of the carapace (upper shell). At the same time the plates jut out more so that its wavy edge at first becomes

more serrated. The very restricted range of this species makes it extremely vulnerable, and through confusion with *T. hermanni* or *T. graeca*, which also occur in the Balkan Peninsula, it could easily become endangered through exploitation by the pet trade. The export of tortoises from Greece is banned, which in theory should ensure their survival, but during 1976 several tortoises were seen in pet shops which were probably of this species, suggesting that some tortoises are still being exported from Greece—although Turkey has been given as their place of origin.

Testudo graeca, the Mediterranean spurthighed tortoise, has often misleadingly been called the Greek tortoise (understandably, because of its Latin name). In fact, most of the tortoises originating from Greece are *T. hermanni*, which are most common towards the north. *Testudo graeca* is normally imported from North Africa, particularly Morocco. More recent evidence suggests that the species is now being imported from Turkey to satisfy a trade demand that cannot now be satisfied from Morocco. It is distinguished from *T. hermanni* by having two prominent spurs on the thighs and the supra-caudal (tail) shield of the carapace undivided.

A Mediterranean spur-thighed tortoise (above) with eggs. Although the regulations as to the size of tortoises which may be exported are intended to prevent over-exploitation, in practise, the export category includes females of breeding age and young adult males

Hermann's tortoise (right, both pictures) is now being imported in large quantities from Yugoslavia, and is being shipped overland in refrigerated trucks

The exact status of populations of the spur-thighed tortoise is poorly documented, although as long ago as 1958 a French investigator, Dr Jacques Bons, now of the University of Montpelier, reported them to be quite common in the under-storey of holly oak woods in the Middle Atlas mountains in Morocco. Still further back in 1833, tortoises were reported to be extremely common throughout Algeria from Oran to the Petit Atlas mountains. In 1969, tortoises have been reported to be common still by the Golfe d'Arzew near Oran where motorists frequently sight them on the roads. However, a survey undertaken in spring 1969 in Morocco suggests that they are now quite rare throughout most of the natural range north of the High Atlas mountains. In the region of Casablanca, the exporting center, even dealers reported them to be very scarce! Nowhere in Morocco were single tortoises found in less than an average of two hours of searching during the most likely time of the year when they should have been basking in spring sunshine and feeding on green herbaceous vegetation where conditions were damp. In some parts of Morocco where there has been exploitation by the trade, individual tortoises were found only after as much as five man-hours of searching.

Tortoises are absent from the hammada regions where the climate is Saharan and only occur in arid conditions by rivers where there is non-coniferous forestation. Their distribution is restricted in exposed conditions by the 0°C mean minimum monthly temperature line and they are absent from mountainous regions above 6000 feet. The scattered nature of records of tortoises from Morocco suggests that the present distribution is all that remains of a formerly greater range stretching south of the High Atlas mountains into what is now the hammada region, although fossil evidence is needed to confirm this. The spur-thighed tortoise has occurred in Quaternary deposits elsewhere in Morocco: perhaps cave paintings by earlier races of man may depict tortoises from farther south although there is no evidence of this from the Tassili frescoes of the Hoggar Range in southern Algeria.

The methods used to gather tortoises in Morocco give cause for concern, and could easily lead to the total extermination of the animals. Most of the collecting is casual, by shepherds and small boys who gather any tortoise they come across in the course of a day. Periodically dealers buy up the tortoises from local collecting centers and take them to Casablanca for export. This form of collecting makes it worth-while gathering very small numbers when the population is thinly spread and can easily lead to local extinction. It is probably for this reason that the dealers have had to extend their collecting ranges farther and farther afield until now tortoises are even being collected from the far south where communications are poor. This is regrettable, for the tortoises from the southern areas are probably adapted to a drier, hot climate and consequently are even less likely to thrive in Britain than the more northerly populations.

Britain and western Europe north of the Pyrenees, with fewer days of sunshine, experience a cooler, generally damper climate than Morocco and elsewhere in North Africa. Even the climate of coastal sun-spots in England is outside the natural range for the spur-thighed tortoise. Because tortoises have been recorded where there is holly oak forestation, from within the vicinity of Ifrane (a winter ski resort in the Middle Atlas mountains of Morocco), two exceptionally mild spots in Britain fall within the species' natural climatic range. It is of interest that two captive female tortoises brought as juveniles from Algiers in 1906 survived in a Torquay garden, in Devonshire, until at least maximum growth was achieved, one of them with record size dimensions. However, although the rain-temperature quotient for Torquay is high and the mean minimum monthly temperature for nearby Plymouth up to $-2.2\,°C$, the similarly damp climate of Tangiers in Morocco is very much warmer with a mean minimum monthly temperature as high as $9.6\,°C$.

Some individual captive tortoises can survive for many years in Britain, with care and attention. Apart from Gilbert White's tortoise, Timothy, and that of Laud, Archbishop of Canterbury, at Lambeth Palace, others have been reported to have fared well. C. F. Moysey's Torquay garden tortoises, 'Panhard' and 'Daimler', lived for at least fifty years. They had hatched in September 1905 in Algiers from a batch of fourteen eggs laid in the previous May. From weights of eight and twelve grams respectively, they increased over the next thirty-nine years to 1.814 (Daimler) and 3.969kg (Panhard). By the fiftieth year, Daimler weighed

2.629kg with a carapace straight length of 298mm (an increase from a carapace over the curve length of 47mm), having ceased external growth after forty-four years; Panhard weighed 4.252kg with a carapace straight length of 365mm (an increase from a carapace over the curve length of 49mm), having ceased external growth after thirty-seven years. New-born tortoises in the Giza Zoological Gardens, Egypt, had a carapace straight length of 33mm. In a series of articles by Sir Peter Eade (1886 and 1893), he and his wife made many notes about the habits of two tortoises, kept in a garden in Norfolk, England, which were obtained from a Norwich street-trader. They showed little evidence of hearing, but their sight was acute and their sense of taste well developed, enabling them to 'discriminate instantly'. Both were apparently males, for they did not fight and showed no interest in each other's company. They had 'good memories', too, for immediately after emerging from seven or eight months' hibernation they would set off for their old haunts as if only a day had intervened.

Most tortoises imported into Britain are, however, less fortunate. Only about one per cent survive the first winter. Of twelve tortoises brought back to Britain from Morocco in 1969 which were kept in captivity by people who were given detailed rearing instructions, five died during the first winter. By the end of the third hibernation, only four emerged in spring 1972. Two males only were known to be still alive in summer 1976. Thus, with care, the survival rate of individual tortoises can be raised above that of tortoises imported in bulk, but even then the proportion surviving the first winter is only a little above fifty per cent.

Testudo hermanni, Hermann's tortoise, is also imported in large numbers, mainly from Yugoslavia, and by 1976 it appeared that many were being transported overland in refrigerated lorries. Most of the tortoises seen in British pet shops during 1976 were of this species, although many of them were brought in wrongly identified as spur-thighed tortoises. Populations of the latter in Morocco are probably so depleted that the demand for pet tortoises exceeds supply and Hermann's tortoise is now imported in large numbers to help make up the deficit. Analysis of the details of the tortoise trade highlights a major problem—which is that the import data is invariably inaccurate. During the summer of 1976, reports appeared

The marginated tortoise is one of Europe's rarest reptiles, being confined to a limited part of Greece. Though the export of tortoises from Greece is banned, it could be vulnerable simply because of its rarity

in the press of large shipments of tortoises arriving at the Channel ports in large refrigerated trucks from Turkey. One driver was fined for being $3\frac{1}{2}$ tons overweight, which must account for at least 10,000 tortoises, since 3000 tortoises weigh about a ton.

The other species involved in bulk trade is *T. horsfieldii*, which is found in the south-west USSR (Turkmenia), in addition to northern Iran, Afghanistan, and north-western Pakistan. It is quite unsuited to the climate of western Europe since it comes from dry, steppe conditions. From 1966 to 1972 an average of 17,000 per year were imported into Britain. Many tortoises were amassed for private gain by no less a person than a former professor of zoology at the University of Tashkent. He was subsequently penalized by the Soviet authorities, who take exception to this kind of behaviour. In recent years substantial numbers have been imported into East Germany, and in 1976, presumably due to a shortfall of both *T. graeca* and *T. hermanni*, several thousand *T. horsfieldii* were imported into Britain.

To summarize, from 1965 to 1975 inclusive,

the imports of three species of tortoises— *T. graeca, T. hermanni,* and *T. horsfieldii*— amounted to nearly $2\frac{1}{4}$ million animals, an average of over 200,000 per year. Although it is quite possible to keep tortoises alive in Britain for many years—as confirmed by some of the evidence we have given—it is certain that only a tiny fraction of these animals are alive today. The bulk trade, which sells these animals mainly to children, is undoubtedly responsible for the depletion and local extinction of tortoises in many parts of the Mediterranean countries.

Britain should pride herself on a more enlightened attitude to wildlife conservation. The trade in tortoises constitutes a black mark that could and should be erased.

ENDANGERED HABITATS

SPAIN'S THREATENED ILEX WOODS

by Anthony Strubell

The conservation of what remains of the Mediterranean habitat is a large and urgent problem, and many Spanish conservationists are at present more concerned with the threats facing the wild areas of Extremadura, in western Spain, than they are with the famous Coto Doñana. Though somewhat overshadowed by its more prestigious relation, the virgin territory in Caceres Province is of tremendous importance since it has retained a large proportion of its indigenous vegetation. The region is therefore the richest in Mediterranean-type fauna in all of Spain—where huge stretches of once-wild terrain have disappeared.

It is a curious fact that none of the Spanish national parks is dedicated to protection of the typical Mediterranean fauna and flora: all the existing parks are either northern (Covadonga, Aigues Tortes, and Ordesa) or *marisma* reserves (Doñana and Daimiel). Given that 85 per cent of Spain was originally Mediterranean in character, this imbalance must surely be put right. The change is especially urgent since the fate of species such as the Spanish imperial eagle, the black vulture, the black stork, and the Spanish (pardel) lynx is at stake. And predictably enough, the last remaining areas of this habitat in Caceres are shortly destined to disappear. They lie squarely in the path of a short-sighted development project that is almost sure to turn into a major ecological disaster.

In Caceres there is still an amazing variety of plants and animals. Huge areas of the ilex, lusitanian oak, and cork oak, with their characteristic undergrowth, that once covered most of Spain are still found there. This explains the presence of 20 pairs of imperial eagles, 30 pairs of black storks, 50 pairs of golden eagles, 100 pairs of black vultures, 2000 pairs of griffon vultures, and an extraordinary abundance of other birds of prey that is unique in Europe.

This splendid bird life is only possible thanks to the complete ecological balance in the area. There is an enormous number of grasses, shrubs, herbs, and fruits that in their turn support the characteristic Mediterranean herbivores and birds, such as red deer, wild boar, hares, rabbits, and crows; these in turn serve as prey for the abundant predators like wolf, lynx, fox, badger, wild cat, genet, mongoose, beech marten, and of course the birds of prey. This thriving faunal community is further swollen in winter by the mass arrival of wintering birds. Numerous cranes, wood pigeons, thrushes, lapwings, and insectivorous birds such as bluethroats, as well as kestrels, red kites, and sparrowhawks, winter in the mild Caceres woods. It is plainly a wintering site of European importance.

(In comparing the fauna of this region with that of Doñana, it is interesting to note that Caceres has 220 species of breeding animals, while Doñana has 183. Important species that in Spain only breed in Caceres include black stork and black vulture, griffon and Egyptian vultures, eagle owl, golden eagle, Bonelli's eagle, and the wolf. This comparison is not meant to detract from Doñana, but rather to give an indication of Caceres' significance for wildlife.)

However . . . well-intentioned development

Cork oak trees with tree heather. Spain's Caceres Province, which is rich in typical Mediterranean vegetation, lies in the path of a short-sighted development project

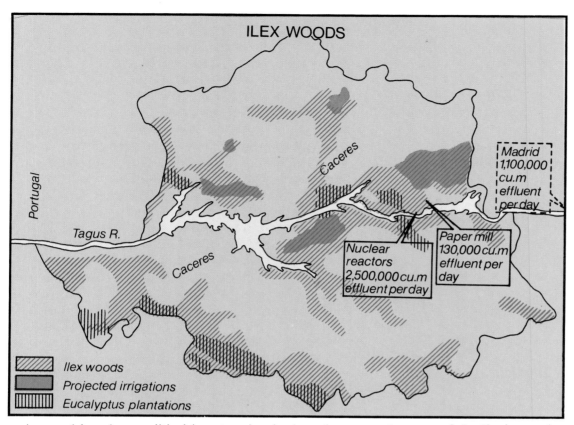

ILEX WOODS

Portugal

Tagus R.

Caceres

Caceres

Caceres

Madrid 1,100,000 cu.m effluent per day

Nuclear reactors 2,500,000 cu.m effluent per day

Paper mill 130,000 cu.m effluent per day

Ilex woods

Projected irrigations

Eucalyptus plantations

engineers, driven by a political impetus aimed at correcting regional differences, have begun to draw up an ambitious plan for the development of Extremadura—but with a total disregard for ecological considerations. In the initial phase, some 125,000 acres of ilex woods will be removed, being replaced by irrigation areas. Another 175,000 acres will be destroyed in order to plant eucalyptus. A cluster of paper mills and cellulose plants are destined to spring up in the area. The province has been declared a zone that will receive preferential industrialization treatment.

Of course, local support has been readily forthcoming since the dream of prosperity came alive in the province—and yet, as in other similar parts of the country, this state of affairs is not likely to last longer than the period during which wages are being paid for forest clearance and canal construction. The illusion of a new-found prosperity is likely to crack when the government stops pouring money into the area. For it is a sad reality that the word 'Extremadura' in Spanish means 'hard land', and to some extent this description will probably continue to be an apt one. The region already has more abandoned irrigation work-

ings than any other part of the Iberian peninsula. The overall losses could be staggering, and not only in the economic sense. A short-sighted, politically motivated development plan, with no sound and profitable returns worth considering, is threatening to destroy ancient ilex woods of incalculable ecological value. Surely it would be more realistic to expand the existing stock-rearing farms which have been successful for centuries because of the fodder supplied by the ilex acorns and the natural grasses? This has been the main human activity in Caceres for many years.

The creation of vast eucalyptus plantations is already causing a major ecological disaster in Caceres province. The last few wooded hillsides and ravines are being systematically replanted with eucalypts, and the thick ilex forest with its dense undergrowth disappears in a few hours, leaving only dusty slopes. The eucalypts are planted so close together that they preclude the growth of other plant species. The lynx, genet, and mongoose disappear for want of cover and prey. The attempts of birds of prey to nest in eucalyptus plantations are usually disastrous. Imperial eagles have tried, but invariably lose both nest and eggs in the first

Savage destruction of ilex woods in the once-wild Extremadura heralds ecological disaster for the region. The eucalyptus plantations which are due to be planted could lead to serious erosion, but it is the wildlife that feels the transformation the most keenly

strong wind. Furthermore, serious erosion results on the sloping terrain because the soil is unprotected from the wind and the rain. Eucalyptus trees also make the soil more acid and lower the level of the water table, leading to the disappearance of local springs. So both the short-term and the long-term effects of planting eucalyptus extensively would seem certain to be disastrous.

But the greatest harm from all this destruction will be felt by the wildlife. The raptors which largely depend on these woods for their hunting and breeding territories will for the most part disappear. The Spanish imperial eagle, for instance, needs about 5000 acres in which to hunt and breed. The destruction of 125,000 acres will therefore destroy the potential nesting areas for some twenty-five pairs. If this vital area disappears, then a rare sub-species will probably be finished off altogether. World Wildlife Fund scientists have discovered that the bird no longer breeds in Morocco, being reduced to the status of a rare winter visitor. And in the Coto Doñana, the eight known pairs barely reproduce due to the high level of contamination by toxic chemicals.

And so if the ilex woods of Caceres disappear,

the Spanish imperial eagle and other important birds will find it hard to survive in western Europe. In the case of the common crane, the fine work carried out in Scandinavia, where the breeding grounds are conserved at great expense, will be pointless if the major wintering ground is sabotaged in Spain.

Yet another serious threat is the degree of pollution that the irrigation and industrial projects would have on the area's water supplies. The pesticides and fertilizers would run off and destroy the last signs of life in the Tagus, the main river running through the area. This long-suffering river is already over-polluted as a result of the frightening total of one million cubic meters of raw sewage that it receives each day in the Madrid region.

Surprisingly, the Tagus still manages to harbor a rich variety of life. Many fish linger on, among them such interesting species as the giant barbel, which is locally abundant. This extraordinary fish can weigh more than thirty pounds. Otters are still numerous and black kites still feed in large numbers on the banks. On some islands and nearby lagoons there are important heronries. It is estimated that there are some 3000 pairs of cattle egret, 600 of night heron, 100 of gray heron, and more than 30 of little egret. And the sight of turtle-eating Egyptian vultures and a thirsty lynx or imperial eagle on the banks is encouragingly regular. Nevertheless, if pollution is allowed to increase unchecked this cannot continue. Already the warning lights are flashing. Analysis of some clutches of imperial eagles' eggs that have failed to hatch has proved that in some places DDE levels are dangerously high. Eggs have contained an average of 6.05 parts per million (ppm) of this lethal chemical— which is liable to cause infertility at levels as low as 0.05ppm. The problem is made worse by the fact that between Toledo and the Portuguese border the Tagus is actually a series of reservoirs. The river's capacity for self-purification and for breaking down chemicals is severely reduced because of the stagnant state of most of its waters. At present, only the surface water contains a sufficient oxygen supply to support life.

In quite another category of danger is the nuclear power station now under construction at Almaraz. This plant will discharge 2.5 billion cubic meters of hot water (at an average temperature of 40°C) into the Tagus every day.

The likely effect on the quality of the river water is hard to guess, but from observations elsewhere one can predict that the amount of algae in the water will increase, and these will in turn de-oxygenate the water, producing methane and ammonia among other things. It is not only the natural environment that is threatened, either, but also the very projects themselves. For example, the enormous Alcantara Reservoir (over three billion cubic meters) may well be totally poisoned by the year 1985.

An arid eucalyptus plantation (above): will it lower the water table? The people of Caceres are seeking a way out of their grinding poverty, but the wide-scale planting of eucalyptus might make them even poorer

The black stork (right) only breeds in Spain in the Caceres

(Overleaf) Part of a nesting colony of herons in cork oak

The great paradox underlying the whole situation—and it is one that needs vigorous emphasis—is that these huge developments, the irrigation projects, the eucalyptus plantations, and so on, have little economic justification. A large proportion of the technicians involved in the schemes are not convinced of their viability, while other people are totally opposed to any uncontrolled development in the area. The cost of the irrigation projects would be staggering— and quite uneconomic because of the poverty of the soil and the great cost of constantly pumping water by means of electrical power.

A quick glance at the balance sheet will show that the eucalyptus plantations have not been a financial success so far. More often than not they are consumed in forest fires, which are fairly common in the dry regions of the Extremadura. If it is a crime to uproot a wood of native ilex trees, with all its wealth of attendant fauna, then surely the crime is doubled when the artificially replaced trees burn down.

The overall situation is thus critical, though perhaps not insoluble. The only irreversible factors are the sewage from Madrid and the Almaraz nuclear power station. But strict anti-pollution vigilance could keep these two dangers at bay. The majority of the other projects are still on the drawing board and need confirmation from the government. Needless to say, one can hardly blame the Spanish government for trying to encourage the development of a province considered to be poor. But Spain must not commit the same ecological errors that are now being so much lamented in other parts of Europe. It is essential to prepare a master plan for the province of Caceres to determine which natural areas should be conserved, and which can be industrialized and turned into agricultural land without important ecological side-effects. The most urgent task of all is obviously to create a national park in the area to conserve the most interesting zones, which in turn implies a complete reconsideration of all the projects in hand.

Some rare and attractive species are being affected by the grandiose development plan: pardel, or Spanish lynx (above); Spanish imperial eagle (right), and little egrets (overleaf)

WORLD WILDLIFE FUND ANNUAL REPORT

In the closing weeks of 1976 the surviving wolves in Italy received complete and unconditional protection. The Italian Government's decree, the result of World Wildlife Fund conservation efforts, crowned a year of successful operations throughout the world.

The World Wildlife Fund's call for conservation of the wolf was backed by two years of intensive scientific research on wolves in the Abruzzi, using modern techniques of capture and telemetry. In all there are about 100 wolves scattered along the Apennine chain.

As in the past the World Wildlife Fund program for 1976 covered a predetermined range of key program areas: conservation of habitat; conservation of threatened species; educational and public awareness activities, and support for key conservation organizations.

Supplementing financial aid to action projects, the World Wildlife Fund continued to be active in tackling conservation problems by direct representations to governments and other responsible authorities. This can be a highly productive field of action.

Project grants in 1976 totalled over $3,000,000, bringing the total disbursements since the foundation of the World Wildlife Fund in 1961 to nearly $24,000,000.

Habitat Protection
The fate of wild species depends on saving their habitat from destruction and degradation. And in most cases conservation of habitat is of direct benefit to mankind for economic, scientific, or cultural reasons. Few areas combine these attributes as clearly as the tropical rain forests, which were the object of the World Wildlife Fund's spearhead campaign for 1975–6.

These forests formed a green belt around the middle of the globe, virtually untouched by man until this century. But already nearly half this belt has been destroyed, according to FAO estimates, and the current rate of destruction is more than twenty hectares (fifty acres) a minute. The threats are over-exploitation of timber resources at the expense of other values, and clearing for agriculture and ranching, for which the soil is seldom suited. Many areas become virtually barren, while floods and silting cause widespread damage because the natural protective and regulatory functions of the forest on water and soil have gone.

A basic task is to survey the whole of the tropical forest belt so that problems and action priorities can be worked out. During 1976 the first area survey was completed covering southeast Asia. Others will cover tropical Africa and America.

Indonesia is one of the countries most rich in tropical rain forest and the World Wildlife Fund has actively assisted the authorities' conservation work for many years. The year 1976 saw the development of a comprehensive program, which will be implemented in 1977, to save key areas and the rich spectrum of animals and plants found there.

Major grants went to the Leuser Reserve in Sumatra, which is the last great sanctuary for orang utan, Sumatran rhinoceros, Sumatran tiger, and the Sumatran population of the endangered Asiatic elephant. In the heart of the forest are two stations where young orang utans taken illegally as pets are re-introduced to jungle life.

The orang utan and the Sumatran rhinoceros also find sanctuary in the Danum Valley in Sabah, Eastern Malaysia, which was surveyed by a team from the University of Malaya. The team commented on the richness and diversity of species found there and recommended the establishment of a national park in the area, which is uninhabited and largely unsuitable for agriculture.

In Latin America the Monteverde Cloud Forest Reserve in Costa Rica was extended with the aid of grants for land purchase to form a well-protected and much visited conservation area. Considerable progress was also made in developing the Montecristo Cloud Forest Reserve in El Salvador, which harbors the beautiful quetzal, black guan, and brocket deer.

In Ecuador surveys were carried out to form the basis for the development of a national park in the Sangay region, which is the largest wild area of the eastern Andes in Ecuador and ranges from 1000 to 5000 meters above sea level.

Rain forests in La Macarena, Las Orchideas and Puracé National Parks in Colombia were the object of conservation grants to help improve protection and management, and support continued for Peru's Manu National Park. In Bolivia a specialist team carried out surveys and worked on a management plan for the Pilon Lajas rain forests.

In Africa Zaïre contains the largest area of rain forest and several very large national parks have been created, in which threatened species such as the chimpanzee and gorilla are found. Vehicles have been sent to help in protection and management.

Rwanda also harbors the gorilla in the rain forest of the Volcanoes National Park. Management has been severely handicapped by the lack of even basic facilities, and the World Wildlife Fund has provided assistance for the construction of buildings for guards. This has enabled more effective patrolling against poaching and illegal grazing, and has also helped to prevent elephant and buffalo ravaging croplands outside the park boundaries.

Ghana has established the Bia National Park to protect rain forests and the World Wildlife Fund is providing the services of a warden, who, apart from routine protection and administration, is carrying out the necessary surveys to produce a long-term management plan. A vehicle and other necessary equipment have been made available.

Wetlands

Like the rain forests, wetlands are also seriously in danger. They are frequently regarded as wastelands ripe for development, draining, and filling in. Yet they are some of the richest biological areas, with important fish and bird populations, and play an important role in controlling the water table in surrounding land. The threat is especially acute in developed regions, such as Europe, and for many years the World Wildlife Fund has provided funds for the conservation of key wetlands.

In eastern Austria support continued for the conservation of the Seewinkel-Lange Lacke nature reserve, one of the most important wetland areas of central Europe. The World Wildlife Fund leases 400 hectares to save them from agriculture and viticulture, and the remaining 600 hectares are lakes, reeds, and swamps. Large numbers of geese, ducks, and waders use the area on migration and for wintering. By leasing hunting rights the WWF was able to protect these birds, and in 1976 the Austrian Government introduced its own hunting law which took over the responsibility.

Austria has another important wetland at Marchauen in the valley of the river March, and the World Wildlife Fund played a major role in its creation as a nature reserve. The riverside forests and ox-bow lakes offer sanctuary to numerous birds, including a breeding colony of white storks. During 1976 a management plan was produced to ensure the well-being of the reserve.

In Britain assistance was given for wetland reserves managed by the Wildfowl Trust at Welney, Ouse Washes, Martin Mere, and Caerlaverock. Apart from providing sanctuary for large numbers of waterfowl, these reserves are playing an increasingly important role in the education of young people and the general public.

Important wetlands on the Tyrrhenian coast of Italy, known as the Maremma, are being managed by the World Wildlife Fund and, as in Britain, great importance is placed on educating visitors.

The most important wetland in Europe is certainly the Wadden Sea which fringes the coast of the Netherlands, Germany and Denmark. Not only does it provide a haven for nearly half a million birds, but it is of crucial importance in the breeding cycle of commercial fish stocks harvested in the North Sea. Nevertheless it is under severe pressure from tourist, military, and development activities, and is heavily polluted by effluent from the industrial regions of northwest Europe. The World Wildlife Fund provides substantial support for the work of the Wadden Sea Committee in the Netherlands which is coordinating studies of the area and running a large-scale public information service.

The Indus valley in Pakistan has always been the haunt of vast numbers of waterfowl,

Rutshuru Falls, Virunga, Eastern Zaire. Zaire contains the largest area of rain forest in Africa, and the government has created several national parks in which threatened species are protected

which frequent the many lakes and marshes as well as the river and its tributaries. There is a wide variety of birds of prey and many other species. Pakistan is a party to the International Convention on Wetlands of International Importance and has designated fourteen lakes as sanctuaries, which are well protected. Hunting laws and regulations have been improved. A wetland conservation expert has completed management plans for sanctuaries in the final stretch of the Indus leading into the Arabian Sea in Sind Province, which holds seventy-five per cent of the waterfowl in Pakistan.

In North Africa Tunisia has initiated a wetland conservation program for which the World Wildlife Fund has provided equipment and technical advice.

Promotion of National Parks and other Conservation Areas

Along with support for existing conservation areas the World Wildlife Fund actively promotes the establishment of new areas, sometimes by exhorting governments, and sometimes by actually helping with the purchase of land.

In South Africa the World Wildlife Fund's affiliate, the South African Nature Foundation, has been raising funds to purchase key areas of the Karoo, which are being turned into national parks under government management. This is an epoch-making development, for the Karoo, despite its great importance as one of major vegetational zones of Africa, and for its wild animals, had not so far been protected.

In the northwestern part of southern Africa, Damaraland and Kaokoland cover an area of 93,000 square kilometers of great scenic beauty and outstanding endemic fauna and flora. Surveys are under way to produce a conservation master plan.

The World Wildlife Fund can claim considerable credit for the establishment in 1976 of the National Park of the Banc d'Arguin on the coast of Mauritania, where some three-quarters of a million birds find haven. Many of them are migrant waders and waterfowl from Europe. The rare Mediterranean monk seal is found in the park, together with dolphins. Aid is being given to establish sound management and protection programs, while assuring the traditional way of life of local people who use the area.

In India a national park was declared at Guindy, a fine natural area within the limits of the city of Madras, which has a valuable herd of blackbuck and other animals.

And in Panama the 3500 meter Volcan Baru was declared a national park, which is of special importance for the quetzal and the primary montane forest in which it lives.

Anti-poaching

Poaching is a perennial and universal problem demanding strenuous efforts to keep it to reasonable proportions. In many parts of the world good legislation exists on paper, but remains a dead letter because it is not enforced. This may be due to lack of political will but it may also be due to lack of personnel or adequate equipment. Poaching pressures inevitably increase as agriculture and settlement develop closer and closer to national parks and other conservation areas.

The World Wildlife Fund has long given high priority to equipping guards. In the majority of cases rough-country vehicles are most needed; not only to pursue poachers, but to deter them by frequent patrolling. A vehicle supplied to the authorities in Niger has greatly improved protection of the western-most population of giraffe, which had been completely vulnerable to well-equipped poachers from adjoining countries.

Boats as well as vehicles have been supplied to Senegal for the protection and management of the parks of the Iles de la Madeleine and Siné-Saloum, while high speed jet boats have been valuable in catching and deterring poachers in the important tiger reserve of the Sunderbans in West Bengal, India, the delta region of the Ganges and Brahmaputra rivers.

Older traditional forms of transport are sometimes more valuable than modern vehicles. This is so in the semi-desert regions of Chad, home of the scimitar-horned oryx and the addax, two seriously threatened antelopes. The World Wildlife Fund supplied funds for the purchase of fifty camels and riding equipment, which enabled improved protection of the vast 80,000-square-kilometer Ouadi Rimé-Ouadi Achim reserve.

Aircraft, especially helicopters, can be very effective deterrents and several have been supplied to African parks by the World Wildlife Fund. In 1976 help was given for the operation of a helicopter in the Tsavo National Park, from where the Warden reported that it had enabled him to suppress most daylight poaching.

Species conservation

The success of the World Wildlife Fund's conservation work for the wolf in Italy was matched by the decision of the Bavarian authorities in Germany to allow four escaped wolves conditional freedom in the Bavarian National Park, when the World Wildlife Fund made available the services of a biologist to keep careful observations of their activities.

Progress continued with conservation of the tiger population, which has been reduced to less than 5000 through its range in Asia, where there were perhaps 100,000 at the beginning of the century. Destruction of forests and grasslands, which were its habitats, plus the increasing impact of ruthless trophy hunting, were driving the tiger towards extinction.

The Javan tiger is critically endangered, and traces of only four or five individuals were found in the Meru Betiri area of eastern Java during a 1976 survey. Unfortunately they are

in an area relatively poor in prey species, for which they have to compete with leopard and wild dog. However, it is hoped that a management plan developed for the area will succeed in turning the tide. So far as is known, there are no Javan tigers in zoos which could be used for captive breeding.

In India and Nepal tiger conservation programs were in their third year and optimistic reports were received from both countries. India, where a census in 1972 traced 1800 tigers, has established nine special tiger reserves under central government direction. Situated in various habitats they have core areas from which disturbance is completely excluded.

A considerable amount of equipment including vehicles, boats, binoculars, and radio networks, has now been provided out of the $1 million pledged to Project Tiger, India, by the World Wildlife Fund. Technical and scientific advice has been provided, such as comment on management plans for the tiger reserves, training in the capture, tranquillization and radio-telemetry of wild animals, and help in establishing ecological monitoring of vegetation and mammal populations.

In a report on the installation of a radio network in the Kanha National Park, the Director, Project Tiger, India, said that at last the devastating annual fires were under control, adding 'Kanha has been saved'.

Meanwhile in Nepal the Government's tiger conservation program, which is being carried out with assistance from the United Nations De-

An Indian tiger in Kanha National Park. The tiger sanctuaries in the national parks are crucial to the preservation of the tiger which had been hunted almost to extinction outside the tiger reserves. In the past fires have been an annual scourge of the Indian forests, but in 1976, thanks to fire control measures such as the clearing of fire breaks and controlled burning of timber, there was no serious fire at Kanha

The International Polar Bear Agreement, which came into force on 26 May 1976, is important because it commits the parties to protect the ecosystems of which the polar bears are a part, including their denning and feeding sites. As a result of earlier bans on killing for fur, trophies, and sport, there are already signs of a recovery in polar bear populations.

velopment Program, the FAO, and the World Wildlife Fund, moved ahead in the Royal Chitawan National Park and the Karnali and Sukla Phanta Reserves, which contain about 100 tigers. In the Chitawan Park a long-term radio-telemetry project is going on which is revealing a great deal of information about the life of tiger, leopard, and their prey. It has also provided evidence of tiger movements which have led to the extension of the park.

The first international tiger reserve has come into existence under the auspices of India and Bhutan, whose Manas reserves adjoin each other at the foot of the eastern Himalayas. The two reserves are now under joint management for the benefit of the tiger and other wildlife.

The first projects specifically to conserve the Indo-Chinese tiger were initiated in Thailand in 1976 with World Wildlife Fund assistance in the form of equipment. This sub-species, which ranges from Vietnam, where it survived the war, to Malaysia and Burma may number as many as 2000.

Another large carnivore benefitted in 1976 from the efforts of conservationists backed by the World Wildlife Fund. An International Polar Bear Agreement came into force on 26 May. This was signed by the five circumpolar nations; Canada, Denmark, Norway, the USA, and the USSR. Denmark, which is responsible for polar bears in the Greenland area, has still to ratify the agreement, which prohibits the hunting, killing or capture of polar bears except for *bona fide* scientific purposes, for con-

servation purposes, or by local people, such as the Eskimos, using traditional methods in the exercise of their traditional rights.

In the Andes the graceful little vicuna, bearer of the world's finest and warmest wool, has been responding well to conservation measures in Argentina, Bolivia, Chile, and Peru. According to the latest population figures there are now some 50,000 vicuna, compared with only about 15,000 a few years ago. The bulk of the present population is in and around the Pampa Galeras reserve in Peru, which has been the centre of promotion of vicuna conservation.

The tahr mountain goats have a curious distribution, with three isolated species, one in the Himalayas, one in the Nilgiri hills of southern India, and a much smaller one in eastern Arabia. A small population of the Arabian tahr survives in the Sultanate of Oman and research began in 1976 with the cooperation of the Omani Government to establish the best conservation measures.

And on the other side of the world work was taken in hand on behalf of the threatened pampas deer in Argentina. One group is already held in an enclosure, but improved conditions and management are vital to building up the numbers. The location of other deer in the wild is being established and their status surveyed.

In Ujung Kulon, western Java, the last Javan rhinos now number over fifty after being reduced to barely twenty specimens ten years ago, when the World Wildlife Fund began its project to assist the Indonesian authorities to improve protection and habitat management. Formerly almost never seen in the thick jungles, there is now an increasing number of reports of sightings, which indicates the improved status of the animals.

Its relative, the great Indian one-horned rhinoceros, is also doing well, with over 200 in the Royal Chitawan National Park in Nepal, and over 600 in the Kaziranga National Park in Assam, India.

One of the major projects launched in 1976 was for the conservation of the elephant. Heavy poaching of elephants for ivory in recent years has aroused widespread fears that they are threatened with extinction in the near future. Nevertheless, no one knows just how many elephants there are in Africa and Asia, and the situation has been confused by the fact that there are still large concentrations of elephants in some areas, while they have disappeared from others. The project aims at establishing a true picture of the elephant situation, and at working out conservation measures.

Despite the heavy toll from poaching, experts do not consider the African elephant to be seriously endangered as a species so far, although they believe that it may disappear from many of its normal haunts.

On the other hand the Asiatic elephant, which is of a different genus, is endangered. It is found from India, through continental southeast Asia, and on the islands of Sri Lanka and Sumatra.

The World Wildlife Fund/IUCN project is scheduled to last three years and to encompass a survey of the whole ecological spectrum of man, elephant, and habitat interactions, including human attitudes towards elephants. It will also include an investigation into the impact of the international ivory trade.

While there was good news about some animals there was depressing news of others, notably the solenodon in the Caribbean and the land iguana in the Galapagos. The solenodon is a small insectivore with a long prehensile snout. Surveys showed it to be right on the brink of extinction in Haiti, with virtually no potential habitat left, and in a critical situation in the Dominican Republic, although conservation possibilities exist if protected areas can be arranged. There is hope that in Cuba, where considerable areas of rain forest remain, the solenodon may be in better shape. It is hoped to arrange a survey there. Meanwhile, proposals for captive breeding in Washington, Frankfurt and Vienna are being considered.

The land iguana of the Galapagos shares the vulnerability of other endemic species to attacks by dogs introduced by man. These dogs, which have gone wild, have been limited to some extent by difficult terrain, but in 1976 they were found to have reached new areas of Santa Cruz and Isabela islands and decimated the iguanas. Scientists from the Charles Darwin Research Station collected the survivors and took them to the station to try captive breeding.

Feral dogs also destroyed most of the young Santa Cruz giant tortoises hatched since 1971, to the great disappointment of scientists and wardens, although fortunately this sub-species

is not one of the rarest.

These incidents highlighted the continual threat of introduced species including dogs, goats, and rats, and also plants and fire-ants in the Galapagos. The Ecuadorian National Parks Service fights a continual battle against them, with considerable success, despite setbacks such as those with the iguanas and the tortoises.

Birds

Efforts over several years began to pay off with the re-introduction of forty-two captive-bred peregrine falcons into the wild in the United States in 1976. The peregrine suffered grievously in Europe and North America from DDT and other pesticides which got into its food chain. Populations crashed, and this fine bird became virtually extinct in the eastern United States. The World Wildlife Fund supported a project established in 1971 at the Cornell Laboratory of Ornithology to breed falcons in captivity. Reintroduction started in 1974 and a

Experts consider that so far African elephants are not seriously endangered as a species, but twins, like this pair with their mother in Lake Manyara National Park, Tanzania, are rare. Towards the end of the WWF's project for the conservation of elephants, it is planned to hold an international conference on the management of elephants and their habitats, in which people actively involved in elephant research, conservation, and legitimate exploitation would exchange information and ideas

total of sixty-two have now been successfully established in nature.

Two methods are used to put the birds into the wild. In the western United States, where a breeding center has been established in Colorado, the young are placed in the nests of wild pairs whose eggs have failed to hatch. In the east it has been necessary to reintroduce young peregrines by adapting the falconer's training methods. Birds are placed in a suitable nesting structure before they can fly and then fed until they can catch their own food, a process which usually takes about two months.

Dr Tom Cade, Director of the Project, anticipates that it will be possible to reintroduce 200 peregrines a year by 1978, and since controls have been placed on use of DDT and dangerous pesticides there is real hope that the peregrine falcon will once more thrive.

Another falcon, perhaps the most endangered bird in the world, increased its numbers naturally. Reduced to only seven specimens three years ago the Mauritius falcon is now up to thirteen, largely because two wild pairs nested on cliffs inaccessible to the monkeys which take young and eggs whenever possible.

In Europe birds of prey are also badly affected by pesticides and general pollution, none more so than the white-tailed sea eagle in northern Europe. Its main range is around the Baltic, one of the most polluted seas in the world, and the poisons which have got into its food chain have caused sterility, thinning of egg-shells, and upset breeding behavior. Furthermore, destruction of breeding habitat and increasing human disturbance in remote areas have taken their toll.

For many years the World Wildlife Fund has

The sea eagle has been called 'the vulture of the north'. Its large wings, which hamper it when flying, make it easier for the bird to scavange for carrion than to catch live prey. This has helped to cause its decline in the heavily polluted Baltic, where those animals which have died, or are sick and therefore slow enough to be caught, frequently harbor high concentrations of pesticides and other dangerous chemicals.

supported conservation of the last few breeding pairs of sea eagles in Schleswig-Holstein, Northern Germany, which includes nest guarding and provision of unpolluted food. More recently the conservation effort has been extended to Finland, Norway, and Sweden where habitat has been saved. In 1975 and 1976 the first successful re-introduction of captive-bred eaglets was carried out. This included taking a German-bred eaglet to Sweden.

Conservation of birds of prey in Spain, one of the largest concentrations in western Europe, continued, by means of feeding stations where carcases are put out for vultures, the purchase of breeding habitat, and public education work to increase understanding of the role of the predators.

Among the birds the cranes are some of the most seriously endangered. Conspicuous and good to eat, they have been over-hunted for generations, and in recent years they have suffered more and more from the draining of marshes and the spread of agriculture. While most of man's activities are detrimental to the life of the cranes, a curious plus point has emerged from the tension between North and South Korea. The natural vegetation in the Demilitarized Zone between them has been able to regenerate and the wildlife to flourish, free of most human disturbance. The Manchurian and white-naped cranes have benefitted and flocks feed and rest in the zone and adjoining areas. With World Wildlife Fund support, the Korean Council for Crane Preservation has been putting out food for the cranes.

A World Wildlife Fund expedition climbed to the roof of the world in Ladakh to find the nesting area of the black-necked or Tibetan crane. What are believed to be the first photographs of the species in the wild were obtained as well as a tape-recording of the voice. The expedition leader, Dr Salim Ali—a Member of Honour of the World Wildlife Fund, who was awarded the 1975 Getty Prize for Wildlife Conservation—later proposed the establishment of a high altitude national park in the area, which also contains the breeding grounds of the bar-headed goose, and a population of the Tibetan wild ass.

Every winter brings a flock of the beautiful white Siberian cranes to Bharatpur bird sanctuary, 200 kilometers south of Delhi. Usually numbering between sixty and eighty birds the flock is believed to be made up of the only survivors of the western population, which breeds in the Soviet Union. Studies are being conducted to ensure good management and protection for this flock.

Plants

Although attention is often focussed on the plight of wild animals or on threatened areas, the public is frequently surprised to learn that probably as many as 30,000 plant species are in danger of extinction. This is rather more than ten per cent of known flowering plants. The World Wildlife Fund is supporting the work of a Threatened Plants Committee established by the IUCN, and with its headquarters at the Royal Botanic Gardens at Kew, England. The committee has already built up a wide network of contacts with specialists and organizations around the world. The Smithsonian Institution, Washington, has already produced a survey of the threatened plants of North America, and in 1976 a similar list was completed for Europe. This showed that at least 1400 European species are rare or threatened on a world scale, although only 100 are in imminent danger of extinction.

Meanwhile work is proceeding to identify the threatened plants of North Africa and the Middle East, and South and Central America.

The importance of plant conservation cannot be over-stressed. Apart from being the whole foundation of life on earth as photosynthesizers of the sun's energy for transmission to animals as food, plants have always been, and continue to be, a major source of drugs and medicines. The potential of tens of thousands of plants, many already threatened, has yet to be examined. And at the same time the production of new varieties of wheat and rice and their protection from disease depend on the constant availability of the gene sources of natural wild species.

Galapagos

One of the first grants made by the World Wildlife Fund after its foundation in 1961 was to the Charles Darwin Foundation for the Galapagos Isles. This international foundation had been established a few years earlier to assist the Government of Ecuador in conserving the archipelago, a thousand kilometers out in the Pacific, which is a living museum and laboratory of evolution.

The Foundation has established a research

station on Santa Cruz island to direct and co-ordinate conservation work throughout the archipelago, which has been declared a national park, except for some already settled areas. Raising funds for the Charles Darwin Foundation and its projects is considered one of the World Wildlife Fund's highest priorities, and it has been possible to help with the building up and maintenance of basic facilities, and the programs for controlling introduced animals and plants which threaten the endemic species, breeding the unique giant tortoises, and for scientific work. Aid is also given to the Ecuadorian National Parks Service, including support for the Warden for higher studies in the United States which will enable him to make an even greater contribution to the conservation of this unique area.

The chief threat to the land iguanas of the Galapagos (above) comes from feral dogs, which have decimated the iguana populations of several islands

Education and Public Awareness Activities

The importance of educating the younger generation cannot be over-stressed. They are growing up in a world in which the problems and threats to the natural environment will continue to increase until human population is brought under control and a more responsible attitude is taken in the exploitation of natural resources and use of technology.

Several national organizations of the World Wildlife Fund have flourishing youth sections which involve the young in conservation activities. Notable in 1976 was the launching of the Nature Clubs of India by the World Wildlife Fund. Limited in the first instance to the western states of Maharashtra and Gujarat—although they contain populations equal to Belgium, France and the Netherlands combined—there were some 150 clubs in existence by the end of the year, and a major effort was under way to service them and encourage their interest in conserving India's still rich natural resources.

The Wildlife Club movement has also been highly successful in Kenya and Zambia, where it has local roots, and in Cameroon and Uganda. In every case the World Wildlife Fund has been able to provide assistance, including books and transport vehicles.

Through a world-wide collaboration by the World Wildlife Fund with the World Scout Movement, which was launched in 1973, the message of practical conservation is being conveyed to over 100,000,000 young people. An annual grant is made to the Scout World Headquarters, which goes towards production of a journal, manuals, and the organization of tests for World Conservation Proficiency Badges, which combine the scout emblem with the giant panda of the World Wildlife Fund.

A regular grant also goes to the International Youth Federation for Environmental Studies and Conservation, which is active among university students.

Wherever possible an educational component is included in World Wildlife Fund projects, directed at the local people. It is unfortunately true that in many cases those who have direct contact with valuable natural resources are totally unaware of their value, and of the fact that they are rare, if not non-existent, elsewhere. Thus in northern Sumatra a special program is being carried out in association with the conservation program for the Leuser Reserve to explain the importance of caring for the rain forests and the rare animals found there, such as orang utan and Sumatran rhinoceros.

In Brazil posters have been produced for a campaign to conserve the seriously threatened giant otter. And work went on during 1976 to prepare for the launching of a massive educational effort in The Gambia, sponsored by the President, Sir Dawda Kairaba Jawara. This included the adaptation of a Renault van as a fully-equipped audio-visual vehicle for presenting slide shows, films, and exhibitions to mass audiences.

To provide educational materials, a special World Wildlife Fund unit has been established. It has been instrumental in promoting the design and production of single and twin projector slide-tape units, including a public address system, called Pandamatics.

International

Effective action by the World Wildlife Fund depends on having the best scientific advice obtainable, and for this reliance is placed upon the International Union for Conservation of Nature and Natural Resources (IUCN), which was founded in 1948. Both the World Wildlife Fund and the IUCN maintain close links with the International Council for Bird Preservation (ICBP) and the International Waterfowl Research Bureau (IWRB). For its part, the World Wildlife Fund provides basic financial support for these organizations, as well as making grants for their special projects.

International Union for Conservation of Nature and Natural Resources

The IUCN is the world's only independent scientific organization dealing exclusively with the conservation of nature and natural resources. It is a union of sovereign states, government agencies, and conservation organizations, supported by six commissions of scientists, planners, lawyers, and other specialists in different aspects of conservation.

With the help of these commissions, the IUCN determines the scientific priorities for conservation action and harnesses the scientific resources needed to investigate conservation problems throughout the world and to recommend and help implement appropriate action.

The World Wildlife Fund is increasingly concentrating its funding priorities within the pro-

Conservation activities at the World Scout Jamboree in 1975 at Lillehammer in Norway (right). Public education, particularly of the younger generation, is an essential part of the World Wildlife Fund's overall program

grams being developed by IUCN. In this way, it can benefit from a system of planning and management that makes the fullest use of available money by selecting the most practicable solutions to the most urgent problems.

Another advantage is the links provided by the IUCN with the programs of intergovernmental organizations, especially those in the United Nations system. The IUCN works closely with a number of UN organizations, particularly UNEP, FAO and UNESCO. Together, these three bodies and the IUCN form the Ecosystem Conservation Group, which acts as a forum enabling its members to avoid duplication and to coordinate their efforts.

The IUCN also screens project proposals submitted to the World Wildlife Fund, evaluating their scientific quality and their merits as projects. In this way, the WWF is enabled to maintain a balance between program activities and responses to particular opportunities and emergencies that arise outside the programs.

Because of the increasing threats to the seas from over-exploitation and pollution the World Wildlife Fund in consultation with the IUCN decided to make them the spearhead campaign for 1977–8. The IUCN brought together the world's leading marine specialists, many of them also involved in FAO and UN Environment Program projects, to establish a comprehensive marine program for the conservation of marine animals, including whales and seals, turtles, and birds, and the identification of areas critical to their lives and to the productive functions of the seas, such as coastal marshes, mangroves, coral reefs, and seagrass areas.

Another important area of IUCN activity involves the Convention on International Trade in Endangered Species, for which it provides the secretariat. This important convention, which puts strict controls on trade, was to a large extent the result of years of work by the IUCN. The first meeting of the thirty-three parties to the Convention was held in Bern, Switzerland, in November 1976 to review its operation and make necessary revisions.

The Survival Service Commission of the IUCN brings together the leading world specialists on endangered species to establish and coordinate conservation programs. An important feature of its work is the compilation and constant revision of the Red Data Books

of Endangered Species which were originated by the commission. These are universally accepted as the authoritative works on the subject and form the basis for conservation measures and legislation throughout the world. Volumes cover mammals, birds, freshwater fish, reptiles and amphibians, and plants.

The overall coordination of bird conservation falls mainly to the International Council for Bird Preservation and the International Waterfowl Research Bureau who get financial support from the World Wildlife Fund on regular basis. The ICBP looks after the Red Data Book on birds.

Since the World Wildlife Fund's aim is overall promotion of the conservation of nature, every effort is made to collaborate with and assist other organizations with similar aims. Among those specially close to the World Wildlife Fund are the Frankfurt Zoological Society, New York Zoological Society, and the Bombay Natural History Society.

Not Just Money
Apart from its financial support for conservation the World Wildlife Fund continually monitors developments and events that might have damaging results. When necessary, issues are taken up with the government or authority directly involved, often in association with the IUCN or other organizations. Thus the Government of Spain was approached over reported plans to develop the Ebro delta, 150 kilometers southwest of Barcelona, which would have had deleterious effects on one of the most important wetlands remaining in Spain. The government responded by declaring a moratorium on development pending a careful study of the environmental implications by an expert committee which was called upon to make recommendations for conservation areas.

The Government of Malaysia's attention was drawn to the damage to the Taman Negara National Park that would result from plans for dams, and at the end of the year there were strong indications that they would be built at another site.

The Government of Turkey abandoned plans to drain the Sultan marshes north of Adano, when the importance of the area as a bird habitat and as a key part of the area's water regime was drawn to its attention by the World Wildlife Fund. The decision was con-

No predator has had such a fearful reputation instilled into everyone's consciousness for generations as the wolf. The grant of unconditional protection to the wolf in Italy is an historic step towards the rehabilitation of this animal, whose important role in the web of life is now being more widely appreciated. It is significant that four escaped wolves have been allowed conditional freedom in the Bavarian National Park, since their escape received considerable publicity, and one was reported to have nipped a child

sidered one of the most significant contributions towards the Council of Europe's Wetlands Campaign 1976.

In response to World Wildlife Fund concern about threats to the green turtle, the Prime Minister of Seychelles, Mr James Mancham, expressed his agreement and said that Seychelles would be pleased to play host to an international conference of interested countries of the area if the World Wildlife Fund would organize it. The proposal is now under favorable consideration.

Pressure was maintained on countries which have not yet done so to become parties to the Convention on International Trade in Wild Species of Fauna and Flora, which is of crucial importance to conservation. In particular members of the European Economic Community were approached since they represent one of the most important trading areas.

In the light of reports that the nine countries would have to accept the Convention simultaneously and that therefore delay was likely, the World Wildlife Fund suggested that where possible domestic laws could already be brought into conformity with the Convention. Subsequently Britain and Germany unilaterally became parties, and several other countries of the community were expected to follow suit in 1977.

The World Wildlife Fund's Fourth International Congress was held towards the end of the year in San Francisco, with the theme 'The Fragile Earth—Strategies for Survival'. Some 700 people from thirty-five countries gathered there to take part in seminars on human population, economics, natural resources, energy, technology, and wildlife, at which panels of experts spoke, including Mr Maurice Strong, former Executive Director of the UN Environment Program, and Australian labor leader Jack Mundey.

The seminars were summed up by Dr Luc Hoffmann, Executive Vice-President of the World Wildlife Fund, in these words: 'We are over-using our resources and we are over-loading our systems, and, as a result, we are in a mess. Whatever we do to reverse the trend it will become worse, at least during the next 10 to 20 years.'

Declaring that the work of the World Wildlife Fund with wild species and wild places was 'at the heart of nature', Dr Hoffmann concluded by saying: 'If the World Wildlife

Fund assures the future of wild places with their resources it will have done one of the most important things our planet needs.'

A set of twenty-six resolutions was passed on conservation developments and problems which were subsequently forwarded to governments and others concerned. The resolutions covered: The Ratification, Accession and Implementation of International Conventions by Non-party States; Trade in Wildlife Products not covered by the Washington Convention; Funding of Development Projects; Conservation and Saving of Energy; Oil Levy to support Environmental Conservation; Support for Youth Conservation Organizations; Use of Anticoagulant Chemicals to Control Vampire Bats; Action to save the California Condor; Spear-fishing; Conservation of the Bald Ibis; Depletion of Porpoise Stocks during Tuna Fishing; Protection of the Harp Seal; Conservation of the Tiger; Conservation of Whales; The Danube Delta, Rumania; Management of the Doñana National Park and Biological Station in Spain; Forest Destruction in Africa; Conservation of Existing National Parks and Protection of Endangered Species in Angola; Protection of the Endangered Fauna of Chad; Pollution of Lake Nakuru National Park, Kenya; Protection of Natural Areas in Australia; Rain Forest Conservation in Papua New Guinea; National Parks and other Protected Areas in Amazonia; Ecological Development of the Tropical Rain Forest in the Amazon Basin; The Future of Palau.

At the closing dinner the World Wildlife Fund Gold Medal for 1976 was awarded to Kunwar Arjan Singh of India for his strenuous personal efforts over many years which resulted in the conservation of the largest surviving herd of swamp deer and the creation of the North Kheri National Park in the area, which is also a sanctuary for tiger, leopard, crocodile and many other species.

The preamble to the resolutions summed up the World Wildlife Fund's approach to the problems of the modern world as follows:

'It is recognized that the fundamental cause of the problems of the Earth can be traced to the growing pressure of human population on natural resources and that any satisfactory and durable solution can only be achieved by bringing human numbers into balance with the potential of the biosphere to support them.

'The present imbalance is leading to the dissipation of the capital of natural resources and often to its complete destruction in irreversible soil loss, the extinction of the genetic resources of plants and animals, the destruction of the potential for production of the land and the oceans and of the self-cleansing capacity of air and water. The problem is accentuated by the prodigal use of resources by the more affluent parts of world society. It often finds its expression in social and political tensions. The Congress recognizes that there is no prospect for long-lasting conservation unless these processes are brought under control.

The Congress affirms its belief in the following:

'Natural resources must be wisely used, so that their potential to contribute to the sustained well-being of mankind may be maintained and enhanced.

'This requires a development of natural resources which makes full use of the potential of these resources but at the same time recognizes the restraints that must be applied if their natural capital is not to be dissipated. Such development must strive to improve the quality of life for all peoples.

'An essential element in any such development must be to maintain, as far as possible, the genetic resources of all wild organisms and adequate areas of communities of wild animals and plants, and of natural landscapes, to minister to the material and spiritual needs of present and future generations.

'Such an image of the future requires that all men and women be made aware of their absolute dependence on the health of the natural world and, especially, that those responsible for decisions develop a sense of ecological statesmanship, and that the coming generations learn to be sensitive to these fundamental issues.'

The World Wildlife Fund

The World Wildlife Fund is an international foundation dedicated to the conservation of nature in all its forms—fauna, flora, soil, air and water. The Chairman is Sir Peter Scott and the Board of Trustees is composed of distinguished men and women, scientists and businessmen, from many different countries.

The main task of the World Wildlife Fund is to raise funds to support conservation projects. This is carried out by National Appeals in 26 countries covering every continent. The international secretariat is at Morges, on the shores of Lake Geneva in Switzerland, and it coordinates the distribution of funds for conservation projects according to their urgency and importance in consultation with the IUCN.

Founded in 1961 the World Wildlife Fund had channelled nearly 25 million dollars into some 1600 projects throughout the world. The actions of the World Wildlife Fund have resulted in governments and other authorities allocating more than this amount to conservation projects as counterpart and other funds. The result has been the creation of national parks and equivalent reserves, and improvement in the prospects of survival of species endangered with extinction, such as the tiger, the Javan rhinoceros, the Hawaiian goose, the vicuna, the Arabian oryx, the aye-aye and the tamaraw.

Parallel with fund-raising and project support the World Wildlife Fund uses its influence in critical situations, often in association with the IUCN, to promote conservation of nature and rational use of natural resources.

The World Wildlife Fund also conducts publicity and educational campaigns to alert the public about threats to the natural environment and the actions necessary to combat them.

The symbol of the World Wildlife Fund is the giant panda, a widely-known and loved wild animal, which lives in the remote mountains of south-west China.

Information about the World Wildlife Fund is available from:

The Director General
World Wildlife Fund
CH-1110 Morges
Switzerland

World Wildlife Fund Addresses

Headquarters
World Wildlife Fund
CH-1110 Morgues, Switzerland

National Organizations

Austria
Österreichischer Stifterverband für Naturschutz
  angeschlossen dem World Wildlife Fund
Festgasse 17, Postfach 1
1162 Vienna

Belgium
World Wildlife Fund Belgium
937 Chaussée de Waterloo B5
1180 Bruxelles

Canada
World Wildlife Fund (Canada)
60 St Clair Av. East
Suite 201
Toronto, Ontario M4T IN5

Denmark
Verdensnaturfonden
(World Wildlife Fund Denmark)
Strandvejen 54
2900 Hellerup

Finland
Maailman Luonnon
Säätiö Suomen Rahasto
Hanuripolku 4
00420 Helsinki 42

France
Association Française du World Wildlife Fund
23 rue d'Anjou
Paris 8e

Germany
Stiftung für die Gestaltung und den Schutz der
  natürlichen Umwelt
Bonn 12
Postfach 0 36 3

India
World Wildlife Fund India
Great Western Building
1st Floor
S. Bhagat Singh Road
Bombay 400023

Italy
Associazione Italiana
  per il World Wildlife Fund
Via P.A. Micheli 50
Rome 00197

Japan
World Wildlife Fund Japan
5 F Yamaki Building
Sotokanda 4–8–2
Chiyoda-ku
Tokyo 101

Kenya
World Wildlife Fund Kenya
P.O. Box 40075
Nairobi

Luxembourg
World Wildlife Fund Luxembourg
Musée d'Histoire Naturelle
Marché aux Poissons
Luxembourg

Malaysia
World Wildlife Fund Malaysia
8th Floor, Wisma Damansara
Jalan Semantan
P.O. Box 769

Netherlands
Wereld Natuur Fonds
Postbus 7
Zeist

New Zealand
World Wildlife Fund New Zealand
P.O. Box 58
Paekakariki

Norway
World Wildlife Fund i Norge
Møllergt 24
Oslo 1

Pakistan
World Wildlife Fund Pakistan
P.O. Box 1312
Lahore

Peru
PRODENA—Pro Defensa de la Naturaleza
Pasaje Los Pinos 164/168
El Comodore
Edificio Alfredo Benavides
Miraflores
Lima 18

South Africa
The S.A. Nature Foundation
P.O. Box 456
Stellenbosch 7600

Spain
ADENA—Associatcion para la Defensa de la
  Naturaleza
6 Joaquin Garcia Morato
Madrid—10

Sweden
Svenska Stiftelsen för World Wildlife Fund
Fituna
140 41 Sorunda

Switzerland
Stiftung World Wildlife Fund
Sörrlibuckstrasse 66
Postfach
8037 Zürich

Turkey
Wildlife Foundation Turkey
Türkiye'de Dogayi Koruma
Vakti
Büyük Dere Caddesi 181
Levent-Istanbul

United Kingdom
The World Wildlife Fund
29 Greville Street
London EC1N 8AX

United States
World Wildlife Fund Inc.
1319 Eighteenth Street N.W.
Washington D.C. 20036

Venezuela
FUDENA—Fundacion para la Defensa de la
  Naturaleza
Apartado de Correo 70376
Caracas 107

INDEX